THE GROWING YEARS

William Sears, M.D.
&
Martha Sears, R.N.

THOMAS NELSON PUBLISHERS
Nashville

Copyright © 1998 by William Sears, M.D., and Martha Sears, R.N.

Published in association with the literary agency of Alive Communications, 1465 Kelly Johnson Blvd., Suite #320, Colorado Springs, CO 80920.

All rights reserved. Written permission must be secured from the publisher to use or reproduce any part of this book, except for brief quotations in critical reviews or articles.

Published in Nashville, Tennessee, by Thomas Nelson, Inc.

Unless otherwise noted, the Bible version used in this publication is THE NEW KING JAMES VERSION. Copyright © 1979, 1980, 1982, 1990, Thomas Nelson, Inc., Publishers.

Scripture quotations noted NIV are from the HOLY BIBLE: NEW INTERNATIONAL VERSION®. Copyright © 1973, 1978, 1984 by International Bible Society. Used by permission of Zondervan Publishing House. All rights reserved.

Scripture quotations noted TLB are from THE LIVING BIBLE, copyright © 1971 by Tyndale House Publishers, Wheaton, IL. Used by permission.

Library of Congress Cataloging-in-Publication Data

Sears, William, M.D.
    The growing years / William Sears and Martha Sears.
      p.   cm.—(The Sears parenting library)
    "Janet Thoma books."
    Updated ed. of: Christian parenting and child care. 1991.
    Includes bibliographical references (p. 267) and index.
    ISBN 0-7852-7208-9 (pbk.)
    1. Family—Religious life.   2. Parenting—Religious aspects—Christianity. I. Sears, Martha. II. Sears, William, M.D. Christian parenting and child care.
III. Title. IV. Series: Sears, William, M.D. Sears parenting library.
BV4526.2.S435 1998
248.8'45—dc21   97–49902
                                      CIP

Printed in the United States of America
1 2 3 4 5 6 7 — 04 03 02 01 00 99 98

Contents

Preface

My dear Christian parents, this book arose out of my own deep love and concern for children as one of God's greatest gifts to us. A child is a gift for us to love, to nurture, and ultimately to return to Him a finished person.

Because they are such a precious gift, I feel that our Creator has given us a divine design for the care and feeding of His children. Over the past decade and a half, I have been increasingly concerned that this design is not being followed. As a result, parents are having difficulty training their children, who are departing from the way they should go. In The Sears Parenting Library I want to convey what I believe is God's design for parenting, and I will offer practical suggestions on how to follow that design.

During my past twenty years in pediatric practice I have carefully observed what parenting styles work for most parents most of the time. Besides learning from my patients, I have been blessed with a wonderful wife, Martha, who is a professional mother. If, after reading this book, you are more able to achieve the three goals of parenting, which are to know your child, to help your child feel right, and to lead your child to Christ, then I will have served my Lord in writing this book.

William P. Sears, M.D.
San Clemente, California

Introduction

The main purpose of *So You're Going to Be a Parent* is to help parents achieve what I believe are the three primary goals of Christian parenting:

1. To know your child
2. To help your child feel right
3. To lead your child to Christ

Each child comes wired with a unique set of characteristics called *temperament*. No two children come wired the same. Each child also has a certain level of needs that, if met, will enable him to reach his fullest potential. Some children have higher needs than others.

Each parent is endowed with a natural ability to nurture. Some children require more nurturing than others, and some parents have a higher level of giving than others. Implied in the concept of a loving Creator is that God would not give to parents a child they could not handle. God's matching program is perfect; His law of supply and demand will work if people practice a style of parenting that allows the divine design for the parent-child relationship to develop.

The term *parenting style* means "a way of caring for your child." Restrained parenting is one parenting style that is earmarked by phrases like, "Let your baby cry it out," "What, you're still nursing?" "Don't let him sleep with you," "Get him on a schedule," "You're making him too dependent," and "You're going to spoil her." These common admonitions from trusted advisers to vulnerable new parents keep them from fully enjoying their child.

The style of parenting I believe God designed for the care and feeding of His children is what I call "attachment parenting," which encourages new parents to respond to their child's cues without restraint. The fundamentals of attachment parenting include the eight baby Bs:

1. *Bonding*. Pray for your preborn baby during pregnancy. Also, unless a medical complication prevents it, keep your newborn in touch with you continuously, or at least as many hours a day as possible during the early weeks. Familiarity builds your confidence because it allows you to get to know your baby intimately.

2. *Breastfeeding*. This is an exercise in babyreading, helping you learn to read your baby's cues. Breastfeeding also stimulates an outpouring of the hormones prolactin and oxytocin. These mothering hormones act like biochemical helpers, which may also be the biological basis of God's design for the term *mother's intuition*.

3. *Babywearing*. Closeness promotes familiarity. Wear your baby in a babysling as many hours a day as you and your baby enjoy. Because baby is so close to you in your arms and in contact with you, you get to know your baby better. And your baby is calmer and easier to care for.

4. *Bedsharing.* Truly, there is no one right place for baby to sleep. Wherever all family members get the best sleep is the right arrangement for them, and that arrangement may vary at different stages of baby's development. Allowing baby to sleep next to you in your bed, especially in the early months, is valuable for busy parents who do not have much daytime contact with their baby. Bedsharing allows you to reconnect with your baby at night to make up for being out of touch during the day.

5. *Believe in baby's cries.* A baby's cry is a baby's language. It is designed for the survival of the baby and the development of the mother. If you listen to your baby's cries and needs when your infant is young, your child is likely to listen to your instructions later on.

6. *Building a support network.* Use the biblical model of veteran parents teaching novices. The support people around you can be a help in building your intuition or they can be a hindrance.

7. *Boundary building.* Practicing attachment parenting according to God's design implies knowing when to say yes and no to your infant and child. This is why throughout this series of books we emphasize discipline as a major part of Christian parenting.

8. *Balance.* Attachment parenting may sound like one big give-a-thon, in the long run it actually makes parenting a lot easier. The more you give to your child, the more your child gives back to you. Yet, focusing exclusively on your baby's needs and ignoring your own is not wise parenting. Periodically take inventory of your overall style of parenting. Ask yourself "Is it working for me?" and "Am I doing what I need to do for my own well-being?"

Attachment parenting early on makes later parenting easier, not only in infancy but in childhood and in your child's teenage years. The ability to read and respond to your baby carries over to the ability to get inside your child's mind and see things from her perspective. When you truly know your child, parenting is easier at all ages.

I arrived at these principles of attachment parenting not only from parenting eight children with my wife, Martha, but also from observing my patients for twenty years. I also have been encouraged by organizations, such as the La Leche League, that advocate similar parenting principles.

Practicing these principles can help you have a realistic expectation of childhood behavior. You will be more observant of your infant's cues and will be able to respond intuitively. As you become more confident in your ability to meet your baby's needs you will enjoy parenting more and more.

Because of the great variability in family situations, some parents may not be able to practice all of these disciplines all of the time. I just want to make the point that the more parents practice these styles, the greater is their opportunity of truly enjoying their child and of claiming the promise, "Train up a child in the way he should go, / And when he is old he will not depart from it" (Prov. 22:6).

What attachment parenting does for you may be summed up in one word—*harmony*. You and your baby will be more in sync with each other; you will become sensitive to your baby.

Mothers also undergo a chemical change when they have this harmony. Because they are breastfeeding and interacting with their babies, they receive more of the hormone prolactin. I call prolactin "the mothering hormone" because it gives mothers the added boost they need during those trying times.

Attachment parenting also gives your child a model to follow when he or she becomes a parent. Remember, you are parenting someone else's future husband, wife, father, or mother. How your child is parented may influence how he or she parents. The lack of a definite model is what causes confusion in many young parents today.

The principles of attachment parenting are especially rewarding for the parents of "fussy" or "demanding" children whom I like to call "high-need babies." We will be discussing the traits of high-need children and how to parent these special blessings.

There is a parallel between a child's relationship with his parents and his relationship with God. The parental relationship a child has in his early formative years has a direct bearing on his eventual relationship with God. If a child has learned trust, discipline, and love from his parents, he will be prepared to transfer these concepts to God. As you study the tenets of attachment parenting, you will see how to apply them to the spiritual training of your child.

In the following chapters, and in the other books in this series, the disciplines of attachment parenting are covered in great detail. For parents who wish to get the most out of this book, read the entire book through once, and you will see how all these attachment tips fit together. By the end of the book I hope parents will perceive these biblical concepts to be a Christian parenting style that is in accordance with God's design.

Part 1

Common Developmental Concerns of Childhood

CHAPTER 1

TOILET TRAINING: A CHILD-CONSIDERED APPROACH

There was a time when a parent's effectiveness was judged by how fast he could hurry his infant through various dependency stages so that he was no longer a baby. A child should not be hurried through any developmental stage, lest he later exhibit diseases of unreadiness. The age at which children achieve awareness of their bladder and bowel functions varies tremendously. Rather than consider toilet training as your accomplishment to be mastered by a certain time, take cues from your child. Consider not, "When should *I* begin his toilet training?" but rather, "When is *he* ready for toilet training?"

Signs That Your Child Is Ready

Most children, especially boys, do not show consistent signs of bladder or bowel awareness until after they are eighteen months old. This is the age at which the nerves controlling urination and defecation become more mature. Also, at this age most children are so

3

overjoyed at having acquired the skill of locomotion that they are too busy to sit still for anything, especially sitting on a hard toilet seat. The two previous books in this series were devoted to an important fundamental principle of child rearing: parents, know your child. Parents who really know their children will intuitively pick up signs of toilet-training readiness from them.

The usual indications of toilet-training readiness in an infant eighteen to twenty-four months old are (1) a desire to imitate Mommy's or Daddy's toilet functions; (2) signs that he is about to relieve himself—squatting down, grunting, a "quiet look in a quiet place" such as a corner; (3) signs of genital awareness, such as a little boy's holding onto his penis; and (4) the after-the-fact confession.

■ Pick a Potty

It's hard for short-legged toddlers to use an adult toilet. Ever try going potty yourself with your legs dangling? To encourage toilet training and toilet using, play the pick-a-potty game. Take your child to the store and let him pick out his own potty. Toddlers are more likely to use what they choose.

Place his potty in a convenient place, perhaps near his playroom. As an added incentive, place a sticker chart next to the potty so that he gets a sticker every time he uses his potty. Once he realizes that he can master his bodily functions, that becomes his own self-motivating reward. ■

Some toddlers go through a stage when they resist any outside suggestions to modify their behavior, especially toilet training. In my experience, toddler negativity has been a highly overrated phenomenon and has been experienced less often in homes where parents practiced the principles of attachment parenting. However, this negative stage does indeed occur in some toddlers, and it is best to respect this and not frustrate everyone in attempts to toilet train during this passing stage.

A toddler often will want to imitate the toilet functions of his older siblings, which should be encouraged. In general, children are mood dependent when it comes to learning. If your intuition tells you your child is not at a stage in his or her development when he or she is particularly receptive to toilet training, back off a while. When you sense that your toddler is ready and willing for toilet training, you may follow these suggestions on how to begin.

1. *Give your child his or her own place to go.* Around two years of age, most children begin to exhibit a desire for order. They like their own shelves for their toys, their own drawers for their clothes, their own tables and chairs, and so on. They also like their own places for their toilet functions. Place an infant potty on the floor next to one of your toilets. Rather than place your infant on his potty chair, simply place the chair alongside your toilet, and wait for your child to accompany you when you go. If you catch your child during this "just like Mommy or Daddy" stage, he may sit on his potty chair when you sit on yours without any urging from you. If your child is not quick to get on his potty chair, you may want to place him on his potty chair when you sit on yours. Most children adapt better to a child-size potty chair than to the more threatening adapter on your own toilet seat. Another

advantage of the potty chair is that it can be moved from place to place in the house or can be used in a car during a long ride.

Initially, your child may approach the potty chair with his or her clothes on. Allow your child to sit on the potty chair with his clothes on, sometimes reading a book or simply using the chair as a place to sit. Since imitation is a powerful motivator at this age, a child often will pull down his pants and sit bare bottom on the potty chair as he sees his older siblings or his parents do. This approach capitalizes on the internal motivation of the "I did it all by myself" stage.

2. *Remove the diapers*. Although diapers seem necessary to protect apparel and furnishings from a baby's being a baby, diapers do diminish bladder and bowel awareness. Uncovered, children learn better how their body works—diapers prolong toilet training in some children. This is why toilet training is often more effective in the summertime when you child can be encouraged to run around the yard without diapers. Most children are not afraid when they see their excrement coming out of themselves, although some pediatricians have reported children's having a "fear of losing part of one's self" feeling. For the child who does not like to be completely undressed, remove his diapers but cover the rest of him with a long T-shirt borrowed from an older sibling.

3. *Teach your child words for his or her actions*. Being able to talk about a skill greatly helps a child develop that skill. Teach your child appropriate words for toilet functions, which is actually one of her earliest forms of sex education. If you are uncomfortable talking about genitalia or toilet functions, the young child will pick up on your feelings. It is amazing how many different terms have been used to avoid addressing toilet functions and genitalia by their proper terms. Give your child appropriate names of his or her genitalia as penis, vulva, vagina. The terms *urination* or *defecation* may be beyond a child. Phrases like *go pee* or *go potty* are much easier. When you notice that she is exhibiting any of the before-mentioned signs that she is about to go, say to your child, "Let's go potty." In that way your child learns to associate the feeling he has to go potty with the phrase *Go potty*. Words make toilet training much easier, which is another reason to delay toilet training until your child is verbal.

4. *Encourage a toilet routine.* Some children readily accept being placed on the toilet at certain times during the day. After breakfast in the morning is usually the best time to encourage a bowel movement. Some people have a gastro-colic reflex that aids in having a bowel movement after a meal, usually breakfast. Stated simply, the reflex occurs when the stomach is full; then the colon is stimulated to empty. Encouraging a child to have a bowel movement early in the morning also starts his day off with a clean slate, and avoids the tendency to ignore his bowel signals later on in the day when he is preoccupied with other activities.

When your child is verbal enough to understand toilet-training instructions, encourage him to respond immediately to his urge to urinate or defecate. Not following these urges predisposes children, especially girls, to urinary tract infections. Girls should be taught to wipe themselves from front to back after a bowel movement; they should not wipe from the rectum toward the vagina, which may transfer bacteria from the stools into the vagina and increase the likelihood of urinary tract infections.

5. *Put your child in training pants.* After your child has achieved daytime dryness for a few weeks, she may graduate to training pants. They resemble ordinary underwear but are heavily padded in order to absorb the occasional "accidents," which are certainly to be expected as she is mastering her newly acquired skill. Do not punish or reprimand her for these occasional accidents. Teach her to wipe up her own little messes, not as a punishment, but to encourage her sense of responsibility for taking care of her body. Little boys often take great delight in spraying their environment, so they may need a little target practice to hit the toilet.

Dr. T. Barry Brazelton has reported a study of 1,170 children who were trained according to their own timetables by a similar approach. The average age for daytime training was twenty-eight months; boys took 2.5 months longer to complete training than girls. Eighty percent of the children were dry at night by age three, and only 1.5 percent of children who were trained by this method were still wetting their beds after five years of age.

Bed-Wetting

Why does a child wet the bed? I want to emphasize that for the great majority of children, bed-wetting is *not* due to a psychological disturbance. For most children, the problem is due to immaturity of the bladder, not of the mind. In order to understand why some children wet their beds, let's first discuss how children normally achieve bladder control.

Infants usually empty their bladders by a reflex called the "bladder-emptying reflex." When the bladder reaches a certain fullness and the bladder muscles have stretched to a certain point, these muscles automatically contract and empty the bladder. Sometime between the ages of eighteen months and two years, most children become aware of this sensation of bladder fullness, which is their first step toward daytime bladder control. The child next becomes aware that he can consciously inhibit the bladder-emptying reflex and hold onto his urine. As a result of this conscious effort, the child's bladder-emptying reflex weakens, and the functional capacity of his bladder increases. When his conscious efforts overcome the bladder-emptying reflex, he achieves daytime bladder control, usually around two years of age. Nighttime control occurs when the child's bladder capacity increases and the bladder-emptying reflex becomes so weak that it is able to be overcome by unconscious inhibition of urination. Delay in bladder control, either daytime or nighttime, can occur if any of these steps is delayed: a delay in awareness of bladder fullness, a small functional bladder capacity, or a prolonged activity of the bladder-emptying reflex. Just as children mature at different rates, their components of bladder control also mature at different rates.

There is often a hereditary basis for bed-wetting, which supports the theory that bed-wetting is a developmental delay in maturity. If both parents were bed wetters, the child has a 70 percent chance of being a bed wetter; if one parent was a bed wetter, the child has a 40 percent chance.

Parents of bed wetters mention that their children are very sound sleepers. In some children the messages from the bladder do not reach the mind because of deep sleep. In some children, bed-wetting may actually be a sleep disorder in which the loss of bladder control occurs as the child passes from one sleep stage to another. It is a known anatomical fact that children who wet their beds sometimes have functionally small bladders and must void more frequently. This fact plus the hereditary basis suggest that bed-wetting is usually not due to a psychological disturbance. In the majority of children, bed-wetting should be considered a developmental delay in one or more of the components of bladder control.

At what age should parents be concerned about bed-wetting? There is tremendous variation in the age at which children remain dry throughout the night. By three years of age, most children are dry at night; by six years of age 85 to 90 percent of children enjoy nighttime dryness. At six years of age 92 percent of girls and 85 to 90 percent of boys remain dry at night. By fifteen years of age approximately 1 to 2 percent of teenagers still wet their beds. Pediatricians usually consider bed-wetting after the age of six a condition meriting correction. What is more important is the age at which the child himself is concerned. Most children sincerely want to learn how to control their bodily functions and welcome suggestions from parents and physicians on how to remain dry at night. There are several ways to help your bed wetter.

1. *Avoid focusing on bed-wetting as a psychological problem* since for the majority of children this is simply not the cause. Understand the development of bladder maturity, and regard bed-wetting as a temporary developmental delay, a nuisance that you must understand, support, and parent as you did your child's other developmental stages. It is important for you to develop this attitude since your child is likely to pick up on your thoughts and feel as you feel about his bed-wetting. If a child's bladder control mechanisms are simply not

mature, outside pressure to force any immature system into functioning before its time is doomed to failure; it produces guilt and a secondary emotional disturbance that may aggravate the bed-wetting. Bladder control in young children is also affected by emotional stress. It is common for children to wet their beds during particularly stressful times.

2. *Early toilet-training habits may affect bed-wetting.* If a child is forced into early toilet training according to the norms of the neighborhood rather than her own developmental timetable, she will have a greater chance of prolonged bed-wetting. Children who are toilet trained according to their own developmental readiness tend to achieve nighttime dryness at an earlier age. This is another example of the basic principle mentioned throughout this book: a child hurried through any developmental milestone often will rebel later against whatever system hurried him.

3. *Teach your child the principles of bladder control* and explain to him why he wets his bed. Your child does not want to wet his bed. He dislikes waking up in a wet, odorous bed as much as you dislike constantly changing his bed and washing his sheets. Older children are painfully aware of the social stigma accompanying bed-wetting, and they do not need further negative attitudes from their parents. Explain to your child how his bladder mechanism works. Draw a simple diagram of a baseball as a bladder, and at the bottom of that ball show a donut muscle that opens and closes to help him hold onto his urine. Tell him that he is not a baby now but his bladder and his donut muscle have not grown up yet and he needs to work hard to keep his donut muscle closed at night.

It is important that your child does not feel he is

a "baby in everything." I am not suggesting you ignore bed-wetting, especially in the child older than five or six, since it is a source of social embarrassment and certainly does nothing to help his emerging self-esteem. As you should do with other childhood behaviors, convey an accepting attitude toward your child. When your child's subconscious desire to hold onto his urine overcomes the full bladder's reflex to let go, he will enjoy nighttime dryness.

A child needs *motivation*. Encourage overnights at a friend's house and overnight camps. Encouraging him to take along his own overnight pad and sleeping bag may relieve some embarrassment. It helps to prepare the parents at his friend's house so that they can be equally understanding and supportive. Chances are they also have parented a bed wetter.

If your child is a prolonged bed wetter, make a special effort to encourage success in other fields of development such as academics or athletics. A bed wetter should be required to assist with the laundry and to strip his own bed, not as a punishment but as a means to convey to him a sense of responsibility for his bodily functions. Placing a large rubber-backed flannel pad on top of his regular sheet may cut down on the number of wet sheets.

4. *A positive reward system encourages nighttime dryness.* Persistent motivation often helps the child develop a subconscious inhibition of her bladder-emptying reflex at night. Daily rewards are more effective than a long-term reward such as a bicycle if a child is dry for a year. A calendar with a gold star or a coin for each day of dryness is often successful. For the older child who wets her bed, pray with her before bedtime, encouraging her to ask God to help her be

dry that night. There is a fine line in each bed wetter between motivation and pressure. Try to sense how motivated your child is to stop her bed-wetting and how her bed-wetting affects her general self-esteem. Then gauge your own support level accordingly. Oftentimes a child who wets her bed is more motivated if she is accountable to a third person such as her pediatrician. A custom I have used for many years for a child who sincerely wants to stop wetting her bed is to have her call me at monthly intervals to give me a report on the number of dry nights on her calendar. You may discuss this approach with your pediatrician.

5. *Teach bladder exercises.* Some physicians recommend bladder exercises to increase the child's functional capacity and to increase the muscular control of his bladder during the day in hopes that they will carry over into his subconscious awareness of bladder control at night. Two examples of bladder control exercises are progressive urine withholding and the stop-and-go technique. Progressive urine withholding encourages your child to drink increasing amounts of fluid and to hold onto his urine for increasingly longer times. Theoretically this increases his functional bladder capacity and weakens the bladder-emptying reflex. In the stop-and-go technique, when a child has the urge to urinate, he is advised to start and stop the stream several times during urination. This exercise increases a child's awareness that he actually can control his donut muscle if he really works at it. Bladder control exercises are usually more productive for children who have difficulty controlling their urine during the day. I do not advise using these bladder control exercises without the advice of your physician. Teach your child to empty his bladder completely. Just before your child goes to bed, do the triple-voiding technique. Encourage him to "go three times" or "grunt, grunt, grunt" while urinating to "squeeze your baseball-size balloon bladder to push the pee out." Many children, tired and in a hurry, go to bed with a half-full bladder.

6. *Restricting fluids after supper* is one of the oldest recommended practices for discouraging bedwetting. In my experience this seldom does any good and is a bit uncomfortable for the persistently thirsty child. Food and drinks that contain caffeine should be avoided since caffeine acts as a diuretic and actually may contribute to bed-wetting.

7. *The shake-and-wake method* is the old custom of waking your child before you go to bed so that she can urinate. If you go to the trouble to get your child out of bed, be sure you waken her completely so she can walk to the toilet on her own power. In order to clarify to your child that you are not taking the primary responsibility for her nocturnal toileting, ask her if she wants you to wake her up before you go to bed. If she is willing, then this practice may be worth a try.

8. *A bladder-conditioning device* is most successful for helping your child achieve nighttime bladder control. Several of these devices on the market are safe, effective, and inexpensive. The device consists of a pad that the child wears inside his or her underwear at night. The pad is connected by a wire to a tiny buzzer that fastens to the child's night garment. When one or two drops of urine hit the moisture-sensitive pad, a beep sounds and wakes the child so that urination can be completed on a nearby toilet.

The device operates on the principle that the stimulus of the child's own bladder-fullness sensor is not sufficient to awaken him fully but the stimulus of the beep alarm is. This beep simply reinforces the intensity of the bladder-fullness stimulus enough to wake the child. By repeatedly awakening when the stronger signal occurs, the child eventually becomes conditioned to awaken to the stimulus of his own bladder-fullness sensor. The device is well accepted by the child because it is his own device for his own problem, for which he takes responsibility. Some children try to play a "beat the beeper" game, attempting to get out of bed before the beeper goes off or with less and less urine reaching the pad. Relapses are common after this device is discontinued, and a second course may be necessary to achieve permanent success. Discuss the use of these bladder-conditioning devices with your doctor.

9. *Consider medications to help your child be night dry.* Drugs do not cure bed-wetting, they simply control it until the child matures out of it. One of the most useful medications is DDAVP (Desmopressin), which diminishes the production of urine at night, similar to the natural action of the child's own antidiuretic hormone. This medicine comes in a nasal spray, which your child uses before bedtime according to the doctor's instructions nightly for two or three months and then tapers off. Many children have a relapse and need another course of this medication. If your child does not respond to the bladder-conditioning device (always try these devices before using medication), the use of this nasal spray in addition to the pad-and-buzzer device may be effective.

With this step-by-step approach, children no longer need to suffer the embarrassment of wet nights, and parents no longer have to endure years of laundry while waiting for their child to grow out of it. For the past twenty-five years in pediatric practice, I have used this step-by-step method of helping night wetters keep dry. This time-tested approach enables at least 70 percent of children to wake up in the morning to a dry bed.

CHAPTER 2

SIBLING RIVALRY

Sibling rivalry is one of the oldest family problems, dating to biblical times when Cain killed Abel. The basis of sibling rivalry stems from comparison, one of the major determinants of human feelings and behavior. Consider yourself. You value yourself physically in comparison to the physical attractiveness of others; you have monetary worth in comparison to that of others. Even in school you were graded on a "curve," and you had a rank in class. Comparisons often result in feelings of inferiority because no matter what parameter you measure yourself by, there is always someone better than you in something. Accepting one's self is an adult goal often requiring years of maturing which, in fact, some adults may never reach. This self-acceptance can be more difficult for a child.

Sibling rivalry is a particularly sensitive problem because a child not only compares himself to other siblings but he also evaluates how his parents compare him to his siblings. This is a heavy load for children to carry. Since anger is the predominating emotion here, you may need to assess how much anger controls relationships in your family. Much of the rivalry you are experiencing could be generated by parental anger in all your dealings.

Another emotion that underlies sibling rivalry is love—the parents' love. Love, at least as the child feels it, may carry with it a fear of losing this love and the unwillingness to share this love with another child. Children cannot conclude that parents have unlimited, unconditional love for each child. When your second child comes along, your first child may imagine that some of your love for him is transferred to the other child. Instead of believing each child gets "one bag full" of love, he fears he has to share his one bag full of love and then his bag is only half-full (or less!).

How to Minimize Sibling Rivalry

Although sibling rivalry is a usual fact of family life, there are ways of minimizing it. There is no guarantee that your child will not get this "disease" at some point despite your immunizing her with preventive "medicine" early. You simply lower the risk. The following suggestions will help you lessen the feelings of rivalry between your children. These steps are directed at minimizing the feelings of inferiority and loss in the threatened child.

1. *Consider wise child spacing.* Parents often ask how close together they should have their children. This very personal decision depends on your individual family situation. I believe sibling rivalry occurs less when children are spaced at least *three years apart* for the following reasons. By three years of age a child is probably weaned from the breast and has received her full poten-

tial of parental input that makes her feel right for that time of her life. The child is able to sense her parents' unconditional love by this time (but only if they are careful to actually demonstrate their love), mainly because she is more verbal in both expression and understanding. The three year old is able to verbalize her negative feelings about the new baby whereas a younger child only can express his feelings by his actions. A three year old can become more involved in the care of the new baby. Temperament is an obvious factor—a high-need child may need a longer space.

Concerning child spacing, parents can take a tip from nature and from God's design. Most (but not all) women who are breastfeeding totally do not ovulate. In some cultures in which babies are breastfed exclusively for several years, siblings are usually born about four to five years apart. Although it is true that having children too close together is exhausting for the mother and encourages more sibling rivalry, some parents feel that this problem is outweighed by the child's having the constant companionship of a sibling near his age; therefore, they prefer to accept a greater degree of sibling rivalry in return for a closer relationship between children.

Parents should be aware of certain trade-offs in child spacing and sibling rivalry. Children who are spaced four to five years apart tend to squabble less, but they also may relate less to each other because they have fewer common interests. Children spaced one to two years apart may be more exhausting to parents and engage in more sibling rivalry, but they also tend to relate more to each other. Much also depends on the focus of the parents—how committed they intend to be in relationship with their children.

2. *Allow your first child to tandem nurse.* Once again, *do not wean your child before his time.* A sibling who supplants a brother or sister at his mother's breast is subject to rivalry. On the other hand, if your first child has been weaned, he may show a renewed interest in nursing. It is quite normal for a two- or three-year-old child to want to resume nursing temporarily when the new baby arrives. This is called "tandem nursing" and should be accepted willingly with a bit of humor. When our fourth baby arrived, our then three-year-old boy briefly resumed nursing, quickly became tired of it, and then satisfied himself by walking around sucking on two bottles for a few weeks.

3. *Practice attachment parenting.* Sibling rivalry is less likely in homes where parents have practiced the principles of attachment parenting for several reasons. First, the child feels right. A child who is secure in her love attachment with her parents may feel less threatened by a new arrival. Second, you know your child. Your intuition has been so finely developed with your first child that you will be more sensitive to the feelings that lead to rivalry among your children and you will anticipate circumstances that promote sibling rivalry. Third, you are role models. By practicing the parenting styles advocated in the other books in this series, you have modeled expected behavior for your child much as Christ modeled for His disciples. By modeling love, gentleness, and touching, your child learns how big people treat little people, which is how she is expected to treat someone younger than herself. You may be surprised, but many children do not know what behavior is expected of them. If a child feels violent, she is apt to act violently to release her feelings.

4. *Pray with your child,* asking God's blessing on the new baby. If your child is old enough to understand, place his hands on your pregnant abdomen, and invite him to pray for his brother or sister inside, reminding him that you really believe God especially listens to the prayers of little children. By teaching your child to pray for his sibling-to-be, you are beginning to model a relationship you expect from him later on, that is, siblings praying for each other. The value of encouraging your child to participate in your "pregnancy prayers" hit home to us during the birth of our fifth child when all our children were present. Within minutes after the birth, our daughter Hayden, then four years old, put her hand upon the head of our newborn daughter, Erin, and exclaimed, "Praise the Lord, Praise Him!" Hayden simply carried over her feeling in prayer for the inside baby to the outside baby.

5. *Prepare for your child for the new baby* as soon as your "bulge" becomes obvious. Let her feel the baby kick. By telling her this is just like she was when she was a baby, you help her identify with the baby inside you. Picture books help clarify misconceptions. Baby is not in Mommy's *tummy,* he is in Mommy's *uterus.* Show your child baby pictures of herself when she was a tiny baby.

Be sure to prepare your child for the time when you go into the hospital. She will probably be more interested in what is going to happen to her while you are gone rather than what is going on in the hospital. Tell her where she is going and who will take care of her. Market the whole idea of separation from you not as a loss but as something special: "Grandma will read you some nice books and do special things with you" (enumerate them). It is usually better to have a substitute parent take care of your child in your own home rather than to have someone care for her elsewhere. This will help alleviate her mounting suspicions that she is being displaced. If a bedroom shuffle is needed to make room for the new baby, do this well in advance of bringing the new baby home. Have her caregiver hold to the child's routine as much as possible when you are gone. While you are in the hospital, communicate with your child often by phone. Bring her to the hospital often to see you and the new baby.

As birthing becomes more homelike in the hospital, siblings are being welcomed into birthing rooms. In my opinion, most children can handle the birth experience by age three and sometimes even younger. Allow me to share with you a bit of pediatrician's intuition. I sincerely feel that if the older child watches and participates in the birth of the younger child, she feels a bond of love and protection for her younger brother or sister, and this bond may have lasting effects on the sibling relationship.

When the New Baby Arrives

Although these suggestions may minimize sibling rivalry, you should expect some ambivalent feelings in your child, especially if your children are less than three years apart. First, understand your child's position. Just when your two or three year old has achieved a comfortable position in the family, someone else comes along to threaten it. It's very hard to sit back and watch a "stranger" become the focus of love from your parents when you still need that kind of attention yourself. It hurts, especially if you feel unloved as a result of losing that attention. Nearly every book on sibling rivalry explains the feelings of the displaced older sibling with a Hollywood-like analogy of a husband's coming home and announcing to his wife, "We have had so much fun together that I'm bringing home another wife and I expect you to share." Although this humorous analogy drives home the central point of sibling rivalry (one's position is threatened by sharing), it is not a realistic analogy. Having brothers and sisters is an accepted norm, and the child sees this as such (whether he likes it or not).

What Behavior Can You Expect from the Older Child?

Older children vary widely in their expressions of their feelings about new siblings. These feelings range from a "no hard feelings" acceptance to overt hostility and aggression. Some children sulk and retreat; other children lash out with biting and hitting in an all-out attempt to evict their new siblings; others show ambivalent behavior, one day hugging and kissing their new siblings (perhaps a bit "too hard"), the next day hitting them. Children seldom verbalize their feelings about new babies; they usually express them by their actions. The preverbal child is especially prone to physical aggression toward a new baby. Expect the older sibling to show regressive behavior; for example, the previously dry three year old may need to go back to diapers temporarily. Expect these anger-releasing antics from your "displaced" toddler.

How to Handle Sibling Rivalry

In controlling sibling rivalry, remember you only can control your children's actions, not their feelings.

Here are some suggestions for handling sibling rivalry after the new baby arrives.

1. *Get your child involved with the new baby.* *Involvement* is the key to the very young child who has ambivalent feelings. Encourage him to be Mommy's and Daddy's little helper, changing diapers, bathing the baby, or doing other similar tasks. This role of helper gradually should evolve to the role of *teacher.* Encourage the older child to teach the younger child. This will profit both of them. The older child will feel older and wiser as he "teaches" his little sister something. The older child also may become a source of developmental stimulation for the younger child. Babies often respond better to the sounds and faces of children than they do to those of adults; therefore, it is quite common for younger siblings to show advanced development. Using your older child as a teaching model is a real boost to his self-esteem and consequently may encourage desirable behavior toward his younger siblings.

If the new baby is fussy and you're having difficulty coping with her fussiness, bring in the reserve troops of older children. Let them assist you in trying various gentling maneuvers. An older child's ability to calm a fussy baby fosters a healthy, protective attitude and is a great preparation for his own eventual role as a parent.

2. *Make your older child feel important too.* Well-meaning friends and relatives may make a great fuss over a new baby and shower him with a lot of gifts. Wise gift-bearing visitors *also will bring gifts for your older child;* but in case they don't, have a few spare, wrapped gifts waiting in reserve. Have a special gift for the new baby to "present" to the older sibling(s). And consider giving your older child a baby doll that wets, has diapers, and can be bathed. If you are breastfeeding, don't give the

doll a bottle—you'll be amazed how readily your older child (boy or girl) will figure out how to "nurse" the baby doll.

3. *Get father involved.* Father, take time to give special attention to the older child. Remember your older child is probably feeling she's lost a lot of Mommy's prime time. This is a realistic fact of family life because babies need more physical maintenance than older children. Dad can compensate for this feeling of loss by really getting involved with the older child and doing fun things with her so she feels what she has "lost" from Mom she has gained from Dad.

As the size of your family increases, each child continues to strive for his or her own identity but may have increasing difficulty finding it because of all the competition from within the family. Take some time out every day or every few days to do something special with each child individually. This special time helps satisfy each child's bid for equal time and gives each the feeling of individual worth.

4. *Encourage your older child to verbalize negative feelings.* The more he can do in words, the less he does in deeds. If he says, "I hate that baby," don't say, "No, you don't." If you deny his feelings, you're denying his right to feel emotions. It is better to express your understanding of these negative feelings and to pursue them and try to turn them into more positive feelings. Allow your child much time and space to approve of the new baby.

5. *Come down hard on physical aggression.* I strongly believe that any overture suggesting an older child is trying to hurt the younger should be dealt with immediately by whatever means necessary to convey the message that you will not tolerate the behavior. Not only can the baby be harmed physically from being hit or shaken, but this behavior models for the younger child that it is okay for an older child to hit a younger one.

Rivalry Among Older Children

Part of the realistic expectations of parenting is that parents often will be called upon to referee squabbles among their children, to judge who is at fault, and to administer appropriate chastisement. The following behavior modifiers are designed to minimize rivalry among siblings.

1. *Encourage the older children to model for the younger ones.* It is a fact of life in families that older children are expected to care for, teach, and model for the younger children. For example, our seven year old, Peter, was having a problem with patience. He was quick to lose his temper and give up on a task if it became too difficult for him. We elicited the help of our thirteen year old, Bobby, to go over to Peter at these times of stress, lay his hand on Peter's shoulder, and say, "Peter, let me help you." As another example, one of our younger children was getting lax in his Bible reading. I asked one of our older children to engage in some brother-to-brother Bible study to model the importance of daily Scripture reading. In addition to a child's profiting from the modeling of another, it teaches family members to be concerned and aware of the needs of others. Admittedly this level of concern for one another's needs does not come easily to many siblings, and a little parental guidance is certainly necessary.

2. *Pray for one another.* A major part of your family devotions can be to encourage your children to pray

for one another. In our family, one child may have the responsibility of praying for the prayer requests of his brothers and sisters, or each one prays for the one next to him and tries to remember to do so throughout the day. When siblings minister to one another they are more likely to get along.

3. *Encourage expressions of love for one another.* The concept of love for one another can be a main focus of your family devotions. You may say, "I'm encouraging you to show acts of love for one another because this is what Jesus asks His disciples to do." Ask each of your children to show at least one act of love for another sibling each day. Hold them accountable for these acts of love by recording them in your prayer calendar during family devotions. This will not be easy, and your children will forget. With encouragement, this can evolve into a real habit and a powerful behavior modifier toward developing good feelings among siblings. One night as we had prayer time, our five year old shared that she felt no one in the family (except Mom and Dad) really loved her. We had a beautiful time together as we explored with her and her siblings how life had been going lately and why she had come to feel this way. We were all convicted and made a commitment that night to find ways for each of us to help this little girl feel the love we have for her. We were glad she was able to express her need.

4. *Minimize comparisons among your children.* This is often the basis for inferiority, which can turn into undesirable behavior among siblings. Praise a child for his accomplishments in relation to himself, not in comparison to a sibling. Each child should feel he is equally special in the eyes of his parents.

An excellent book on this subject is *Siblings Without Rivalry: How to Help Your Children Live Together So You Can Live Too* by Adele Faber and Elaine Mazlish (see Bibliography).

Child Spacing and Natural Family Planning

For a variety of socioeconomic reasons, couples may wish to limit the size of their families or wisely space their children. In this section the options of family planning open to Christian couples are presented, especially following the birth of a new baby. The term *conception control* is more accurate for the Christian couple than birth control since any method that prevents the birth of a baby after conception has occurred is not an option for them. The following information should help you make an informed choice.

Oral contraceptive—"the pill." Although it is perhaps the most effective method of artificial conception control, the pill is also one of the least safe. Many women experience side effects because the hormones contained in the pill interfere with their natural hormonal functions. As more and more information is known about the real and potentially harmful effects of the pill, this form of contraception is gradually becoming less attractive. If the pill fails to suppress ovulation, it then prevents implantation of the fertilized ovum. In this case the pill produces an abortion. Breastfeeding is usually not successful or advisable while you are taking the pill because of the hormonal interference (in some women the amount of milk produced will decrease even with the minimal dose pill) and the possibility of excessive hormones passing into the baby's system. The intricate workings of a woman's hormonal system is one of God's most remarkable creations. In my opinion, artificially manipulating these hormones in order to suppress ovulation or implantation is not only medically unsafe but is not in accordance with God's admonition to regard our bodies as temples of the Holy Spirit (1 Cor. 3:16; 6:19).

The intrauterine device (IUD). The IUD is a coil-like device that is inserted into the uterus by a physician. There can be medical complications such as infection, perforation of the uterus, and hemorrhage. The real issue for the Christian is how the IUD works. The current IUDs are abortifacients, that is, they cause abortions by preventing the implantation of fertilized eggs into the uterine walls. Therefore, I do not recommend IUDs.

Diaphragm and spermicidal foam and jelly. These methods are less effective and unattractive because they put a damper on the spontaneity of sex, and sometimes they cause allergy or infection. However, they are efficient methods of contraception.

Condoms. Condoms are way down on this list of options. A condom alone is not always effective and should be used in conjunction with a diaphragm and spermicide in the female. Males often choose not to use condoms because they feel they lessen the pleasure of intercourse.

None of these methods of conception control is perfect. The pill and IUD are often medically unsafe or morally wrong, and the rest may be ineffective or unattractive.

Sterilization. As a Christian physician, I am disappointed to see Christian couples decide upon sterilization without prayer and consultation. I personally believe that voluntary sterilization (unless for certain medical conditions) is unwise. Before considering tubal ligation or vasectomy, consider the following: You are making a permanent decision based on your lifestyle and your feelings *at the present time*. You cannot predict how you may feel or how your family situation will be in the future. I have counseled many couples who wish to have sterilization reversed because their lifestyle, priorities, financial situation, or material situation changed, even though at the time they made the decision they were "certain" they didn't want any more children.

The medical safety of sterilization, especially vasectomy, is open to question. Increasing scientific evidence suggests that some males, following vasectomies, develop sperm antibodies that may lead eventually to diseases of the immune system. Reported in *Medical World News,* September 25, 1988, a study at Boston University presented by the Society for Epidemiological Research showed that men who have vasectomies are three times more likely to develop prostate cancer than other men (prostate cancer accounts for 21 percent of all new cancers in American men and for 11 percent of all cancer deaths in American men). Similar results were reported in the *British Journal of Cancer,* March 1988.

Natural child spacing method. Scientific studies have shown that breastfeeding is a 95 percent effective method of conception control for at least a year after childbirth but *only if all the rules of the game are followed.* The act of suckling and the process of lactation results in a continuation of the hormonal state of pregnancy with the result that ovulation and menstruation do not occur. However, here a word of caution needs to be added. Breastfeeding is an effective method of contraception *only* if performed according to the techniques suggested in Sheila Kippley's book *Breastfeeding and Natural Child Spacing*.

1. Total breastfeeding-on-demand with a complete openness to night nursings and without the use of pacifiers or bottles.
2. Delayed supplements of solids and other liquids until the baby is six months old, and then only in minimal quantities.
3. Encouraging frequent, vigorous nursings without regard for the clock or the calendar.

In nearly every case where the mother has reported that "it didn't work," there was usually a breakdown in one or more of these requirements, usually the most common being not welcoming the baby into the family bed and discouraging night nursings. The amount of suckling stimulation necessary to suppress ovulation varies greatly from mother to mother, which is why some women conceive although they apparently follow all the rules. However, if couples follow the suggestions of the continuum concept of Christian parenting as discussed in the first book in this series, the wife is unlikely to conceive while breastfeeding until her menstrual cycle returns.

Studies have shown the following results in breastfeeding mothers: (1) the average length of lactation amenorrhea (no menstruation and therefore no fertility) is 14.6 months (the range is from two to thirty months); (2) 95 percent of these mothers do not ovulate before their first periods following childbirth and are not fertile until after their first periods occur; and (3) in 5 percent of mothers, fertile ovulation occurs before menstruation but usually not before the twelfth month.

Natural family planning method (NFP). These mothers who ovulate before their first periods are potentially fertile, even though they are completely breastfeeding their infants. Take heart though. There is still another method of conception control for these women, and that is the Natural Family Planning Technique. It consists of observing the following signs.

Examine your cervical mucous daily. At the midpoint of a woman's cycle she is fertile, and this fertility is heralded by the appearance of a stringy, egg-white type of mucous coming from the cervix. This mucous is readily detectable at the entrance to the vagina. The onset of fertility is also characterized by a slight rise in body temperature in the morning.

Complete details on fertility awareness by detecting the cervical mucous and increased body temperature are given in the references listed in the natural family planning section in the Bibliography.

Natural family planning is a way of loving, not just a method of conception control. If this method is used correctly, studies have shown the combination of complete breastfeeding and fertility awareness to be nearly 100 percent effective. As a result, children can be spaced two to three years apart. One drawback to this method is that abstinence is advised when the woman is fertile, which is also usually at the height of her sexual interest. The dilemma could be solved by using a combination of diaphragm, spermicides, and condom during this fertile time, but then it's no longer *natural* family planning with the element of trusting God to be the One who is ultimately in charge of blessing you with new life. NFP does require a certain amount of self-discipline for husband and wife—it is that element of sacrifice (see Rom. 12:1–2) that makes NFP so special in building up the marriage. I highly encourage you to learn more by reading *The Art of Natural Family Planning* by Dr. John Kippley. This technique requires a woman to understand how her own body works sexually and hormonally.

For more information on informed choices of conception control and Natural Family Planning, write to The Couple to Couple League, P.O. Box 111184, Cincinnati, Ohio 45211.

CHAPTER 3

DISCIPLINE

Father, I acknowledge You as the author of all discipline. I accept the responsibility You have given me to discipline my child. Your instructions are clear, but my spirit is weak. Discipline me that I may discipline my child and by so doing return him and his children and his children's children to You, their almighty Father. Amen.

Parents have become accustomed to thinking about discipline as punishment—some external force that is applied to a child to keep him or her in line. Chastening is indeed a part of Christian discipline, but a minor part. (See Chapter 6 for how chastening differs from punishment.) If as Christian parents you sincerely want to discipline your child, your most effective discipline is to create such an attitude within your child and an atmosphere within your home that chastening seldom becomes necessary. But when chastening does become necessary, you must administer it appropriately. Dwell upon this thought for a minute: This may mean changing your attitude toward discipline so you consider how to avoid the necessity of chastening rather than considering how to chasten. In my opinion, too much emphasis is placed on the rod, especially by Christian writers. In the following section the concept of discipline will be built upon as a positive direction from within the child rather than an external force from outside the child. Christian parents will be taught how to chasten their children in such a way that they will see that the Christian approach to solving problems and healing relationships is a practical way of life.

Laying the Foundation—
Discipline Begins at Birth

Parents usually begin to think about the how-tos of discipline when their children are about two years old because that is when most power struggles between parent and child begin. During their babies' fifteen-month checkup, parents may ask, "Can we discuss discipline now?" I often reply, "You began disciplining your child from the moment of birth." In reality, discipline is not one isolated part of the total package of child rearing. Everything you do with your child from the moment of his or her birth will play a part in discipline.

Four basic building blocks form the foundation for discipline and spiritual training of the child: basing discipline on Scripture, providing a spiritual model, knowing your child, and helping your child feel right. God, our Father, has directed parents to do two things for their children: to teach and to discipline. *Teaching* and *disciplining,* as used in the Bible, are similar terms, but they differ in degree. *Teaching* means to impart God's Word to your children. *Disciplining* goes one step further—it imparts God's Word to your children to such a degree that His Word becomes part of each child's inner self, his inner controls, his base of operations. In short, to discipline a child means to instill a sense of direction.

Today's parents are bombarded with a flurry of theories and books on how to discipline. As a result, many sincere parents flounder in a sea of uncertainty. There is only one way for Christian parents to discipline their children, and that is God's way. Go to His Book and analyze His specific instructions on how to discipline your children.

Proverbs 22:6 is the master verse of Christian discipline: "Train up a child in the way he should go, / And when he is old he will not depart from it." The book of Proverbs is noted for short verses with deep meaning. Dig into this verse now and discover what God is saying to you. *Train* means "bringing into submission." God is reminding you of your awe-inspiring responsibility to discipline your children. These are words of authority and commitment to get in there and work at it. In essence, God is saying: "Parents, take charge of your children." The instruction is the same for all ages, infancy through adolescence; discipline is a constant commitment until the child is ready to leave home.

There are various interpretations of the phrase, "in the way he should go." Does God mean he should go toward the general plan He has for all children to keep His commandments and follow His teaching? Or does God imply a more specific plan, one that is according to your child's inherent temperament and characteristics? Biblical scholars suggest the latter interpretation. Each child has an individual bent or "way" and an individual plan. What God is saying to you is to know your child, be tuned in to his individual bent, keep your radar system attuned to the direction he should take, and keep him focused in that direction *(which may not necessarily be the direction you want for him)*. This concept may be hard for parents to understand: "How do we know what destiny God has for our child?" The concept of knowing your child will be discussed in detail later on.

Some parents are disappointed when they really have trained their children, yet they seem to depart during the early teen years when they are deciding whether or not to accept their parents' values as their own. Parents, don't despair. For some children, there may be a longer time gap in the middle of the proverb: "in the way he should go . . . when he is old he will not depart." Some children temporarily stray from the way they should go, but because of an indelible Christian foundation imprinted upon them, they find their way again and do not depart from it.

The next biblical concept, and one which is very difficult for most parents to understand, is that within the child's nature is a bent toward good and a bent toward evil. It is up to Christian parents to unbend their children's tendency toward evil. The following Scriptures make this concept very clear: "I was brought forth in iniquity, / And in sin my mother conceived me" (Ps. 51:5); and "Foolishness if bound up in the heart of a child; / The rod of correction will drive it far from him" (Prov. 22:15). Proverbs 29:15, "A child left to himself brings shame to his mother," also reinforces the concept that a child has an inherent bent toward evil. This concept is not in keeping with the secular view that a child should be left alone to decide for himself the way he should go. A child left without direction probably will wander. It is like throwing a child into a stream without first teaching him how to swim. If a child has not been trained to swim against the current, he will be swept along downstream by the prevailing current of the world.

In the preceding scriptural passages, God gave the following guidelines for effective discipline:

1. Make a commitment to discipline your child.
2. Assume authority; take charge of your child.
3. Know your child.
4. Recognize the evil bent in your child.
5. Expect a high probability of success if you follow these guidelines.

Now take these biblical guidelines and create an approach to effective discipline applicable to practical life situations. Consider the growth of the disciplined child, a child with direction, to be analogous to a tree's growing to bear fruit. The soil is the foundation of disciplined parents, and the trunk contains the principles of attachment parenting, improving the child's behavior. Evil influences bend the child one way and good influences bend the child the other.

Provide a Spiritual Model

Make Jesus Christ Lord of Your Lives

You cannot give to your children what you do not have yourselves. It is difficult, if not impossible, to impart a sense of direction to your children if you do not have direction. Your library may be filled with books about discipline, and you may preach many sermons to your children, but your example, what you are through the eyes of your children, will always be their best teacher.

Make a commitment that Christian discipline is a top priority. I will stress continually this term *commitment* because it forms the basis for all of parenting. You are well on your way to effective Christian discipline of your child if you love and fear your God and walk in His ways.

Know Your Child

To discipline your child, you must know your child. To train a child in the way he should go, you must know which way he should go. Almost all parents truly love their children; however, parents vary in the degree to which they *know* their children. The attachment style of parenting helps you to know your child better. For review, the essentials of attachment parenting are prenatal bonding; bonding and rooming-in at birth; father involvement in baby's care and spiritual leadership; unrestricted breastfeeding with infant-led weaning; a strong mother-infant attachment; nighttime parenting; gentling the high-need baby; unrestrained response to baby's cries; lots of touching, eye-to-eye contact, and focused attention; and daily prayer for wisdom to know your child.

What do parenting styles have to do with discipline? During my twenty years in pediatrics, I have noticed that parents who have practiced attachment parenting do indeed have fewer discipline problems with their children. Attachment parenting provides the best conditions for parents to really know their children.

I've noticed that parents who practice these attachment tips have the following characteristics as "disciplinarians": (1) they are more observant of their infants' actions; (2) they respond intuitively to their infants' cues; (3) they are more confident in the appropriateness of their responses; (4) the fathers are more involved in parenting; (5) they are sensitive to the feelings and circumstances that promote misbehavior; (6) they know how to convey expected behavior to their children; (7) they have more realistic expectations of childhood behavior in general; (8) they have a wider acceptance of what is normal for *their* children's behavior and are less provoked to anger; (9) they seek prayer and counsel when the going gets tough; (10) they learn the true meaning of giving of themselves; and (11) they enjoy their children more.

The family functions as a father-mother-baby *unit*. It is easier to discipline part of yourself because you know this self (baby) better. It's so beautiful to watch a mother, father, and baby who are in harmony with one another. Whenever I see this harmony in my office, I can't help feeling that surely this is God's design for the parent-child relationship. I believe God designed discipline to flow naturally from this inner harmony; discipline shouldn't be considered a list of methods of external forces suggested by some third-party adviser.

One day I was watching a mother respond intuitively to her child. The two were in harmony with each other. I said to her, "You're a good disciplinarian." Surprised, she responded, "But I don't spank my child." I went on to explain that "disciplinarian" implied the relationship of trust and harmony between her and her child.

Help Your Child Feel Right

Children who are the products of attachment parenting are easier to discipline because as infants they feel right, and infants who feel right are more likely to act right. This inner feeling of rightness is the beginning of a baby's self-esteem, and a child's behavior usually mirrors his or her feeling of self-esteem. This style of parenting also allows a mutual trust to develop between caregiver and child. Admittedly, the ease with which you can discipline your child is to a great extent determined by his or her temperament. However, a baby who has this inner feeling of rightness seems to have a greater receptivity to being directed, as if direction, or discipline, reinforces this feeling. An inner feeling of unrightness within a child makes him less receptive to direction either from within or outside himself and accounts for the frustration of parents who state, "We just can't get through to him."

This next statement may surprise you, but I feel that the most important stage of discipline is the period from birth to one year of age. During this period you are developing sensitivity to your baby, getting to know him, maturing your intuition, and helping your baby feel right. This is the period in which you are maturing in your attitudes toward the whole process of child rearing, and every little interaction you have with your baby carries over into discipline. Dr. James Dobson has made an important point that discipline is a balance between love and control. Being open to your baby during his first year allows this control to develop naturally during his second year. Before you can control your child (in the biblical sense of guiding him), you must first be open to him. Control will flow naturally from a foundation of knowledge of your child and openness to him. In the first few months you will find that being open to your baby means that you anticipate and respond to her needs promptly and totally. You are there for your baby unreservedly, giving her what she wants when she wants it, building love and trust. And all is well—no problem—harmony.

Around the third or fourth month there is a slight shift in the balance. Your baby can now become bored because developmentally she is ready for more than just being held and fed; she can become frustrated because her mind drives her to do things her body isn't ready to do yet. The cry that your baby uses to signal her boredom or frustration will be different from the hunger, pain, or "need to be held" cry, and you will still respond as quickly as possible but gradually you will learn that these cries don't require the "red alert" response from you. You don't have to drop everything the instant she signals; you find you can buy a little time (one or two minutes, then three or four) by using your voice to reassure that you are here and you are coming. Your baby learns she can wait, and you both learn just how long. This all happens gradually, without any calculation, but one day, when she's six months old, you realize that your responses are considerably slower now than they were at six days or six weeks. It would simply not be healthy if you were still trying to be so promptly and totally "there" for your six to nine month old as you were in the first few months.

In the next stage of child development, the toddler years, you will build upon this foundation toward widening the scope of Christian discipline, that of guiding the child.

■ Shaping vs. Control

Christian parents often confuse being in charge with being in control. A control style of parenting regards discipline as something you do *to* a child instead of what you do *with* a child.

Discipline is more of having the right relationship with your child than striving for the right techniques. We control situations, not people. Children who are controlled behave more out of fear of punishment than desire to please. They develop no inner controls. Once the controllers' backs are turned, the children run wild.

Think of discipline more as shaping a child's behavior than trying to control the child. You can't control the color of the flower or when it blooms, but you can prune the plants and pick the weeds so the flower grows better.

Throughout this series of books, we have tried to give parents gardening tools to help them shape their child's behavior, not control it; the ultimate goal being to teach children how to control themselves. ∎

Disciplining the Child One to Two Years Old

In the preceding section you learned how to lay the foundation for effective discipline in your infant's first year of life by (1) knowing your infant, (2) helping him feel right, and (3) seeing that he securely trusts you as his caregivers. Building a strong foundation on these elements in his first year gives you something on which to build a concept of disciplining him as a toddler. Without this foundation, discipline will evolve into a science of methods. With this foundation, you naturally and intuitively will guide your child instead of reacting emotionally to his actions.

By the time a child is twelve months old the roles of both infant and parent take on a new direction. In the first year, your role is primarily that of caregiver. This role certainly continues, but in the second year it broadens into the additional roles of authority figure and designer of your child's environment. In the first year your child's environment is mainly your arms, your breasts, and your bed. In the second year your child's environment widens through his acquiring two new abilities: locomotion and speech. As the roles of parent and child take on a broader perspective, so does the concept of discipline. In the first year, discipline means primarily conveying love and security to your infant and learning to know him. In the second year, discipline also requires guidance. The following discussion will center on two main features of guiding your child: (1) how to develop realistic expectations and knowledge of normal or usual toddler behavior in general, and of your child's behavior in particular; and (2) how to modify your toddler's bent toward undesirable behavior and channel his energies toward desirable behavior.

At this point, take inventory of what your one year old is like as a person. When I ask parents to tell me about their child at the one-year checkup, they may say, "He is beginning to walk, he plays with blocks, he feeds himself," and so on. This is not the kind of answer I am hoping for. They have told me what the child *does,* not what he *is.* Other parents may say, "He likes to be held a lot; he is most happy when he . . . ; his favorite toy is . . . ; he loves to roll on his daddy's chest . . . ; his mood is generally pleasant, but he has his fussy times at the end of the day. I guess he is just tired. I've learned to handle these fussy moments." Those are the cue words I'm looking for: "he likes," "he feels," "I feel," "I know when he . . ." These parents have a head start toward effective discipline because they know their child.

Since discipline begins with knowing your child, use the following checklist to take inventory of how well you know your one year old:

- What makes your baby most happy, laughing and cooing?
- What makes your baby most unhappy, crying or sad?
- What parent-child play activity does he or she like best (playing peekaboo, crawling on Dad's chest)?
- What are your baby's most noticeable cues that he or she needs something?
- Are you confident that you recognize and respond appropriately to your baby's cues, such as crying, gesturing, body tone, etc.?
- Does your response to your baby's cues make you both feel better?
- Does your baby feel right most of the time?
- Are you comfortable helping your baby feel right, such as comforting him when he or she is fussy?
- Do you enjoy being with your baby most of the time?
- Generally speaking, do you enjoy being a parent?
- Do you pray and seek counsel when problems arise either in your marriage relationship or in your parent-child relationship?
- Do you pray for your child daily?

This inventory is a general measure of how finely tuned your communication network is with your baby. If you have answered with more negatives than positives, please pray and seek counsel at this stage of your parent-child relationship so that you can make the subsequent stage of disciplining your toddler more effective.

■ Teaching Your Child a Sense of Responsibility

One of the ways children develop self-confidence is to feel useful and helpful in doing their share of household duties. Try these tips:

Enter the workforce early. Beginning around age two, children can do small jobs around the house. Our two year old, Lauren, had a thing about napkins, so we gave her the dinnertime job of putting napkins at each place-setting. A mother in our practice told us: "I couldn't keep our three year old away from the vacuum cleaner, so I gave him the job of vacuuming the family room. He kept busy and I got some work out of him." By three years of age, a child can be taught to clean sinks and tubs, using a sponge. Young children love to scrub. Threes and fours love to sort laundry into darks and whites. At five a child can help with the dishes. By seven, a child can help plan, shop for, and prepare an evening meal. By giving children a sense of responsibility for their own nutrition, they are more likely to eat what they make.

Give special jobs. "Special" is your magic word. It gets results. Perhaps the child infers "I must be special because I get a special job." A four to five year old can have preassigned chores, with reminders, of course. To put some order in our busy house, we announce: "It's tidy time." Try assigning one room for each child to tidy up. Children of all ages suffer a bit of work inertia, especially as tasks lose their fun appeal. To get your children started, work *with* them. As an added incentive use the "when . . . then" technique: "*When* you finish tidying your room, *then* you can go outside and play."

Create job charts. During a family meeting, list the jobs to be done, and let each child choose and rotate if they want. We divide jobs into paying (extra-credit jobs they can earn money for) and nonpaying (those that are naturally expected of the children for the privilege of living in the home). It is best to pay immediately after the work is responsibly done, since children are immediate-reward oriented. Between five and ten, children can make the connection that with increasing privileges come responsibilities. ■

Have Realistic Expectations of Normal Toddler Behavior

Many first-time parents do not have a clear understanding of what is normal or usual toddler behavior, and they may therefore interpret certain behaviors as "bad." Not understanding and accepting normal toddler behavior may lead to being harsh when you should be gentle, and restricting when you should be channeling. This is part of parental maturity that is necessary for effective discipline. The more children you have, the more your concept of normality will broaden and the more your acceptance level will widen. As a father of eight this is my first survival tip to you.

Locomotion widens your child's environment around age one. The ability to walk brings an insatiable appetite to explore. When his desire to explore matches his locomotor capabilities, he is in balance. When his desire to explore is greater than his capabilities to get there, he is out of balance. Also, when desire is greater than capability, his inner frustrations may be manifested by tantrumlike behavior. This imbalance results in *ambivalence*, one of the most normal and noticeable characteristics of a toddler. For example, watch toddlers in a park with limitless space to roam. A few will zip away from Mommy a long distance to explore. A few others will cling to Mommy because they seem threatened. Some toddlers will run off a short distance but will look back periodically to home base to be sure Mommy is still there.

A characteristic of child development, especially that of a toddler, is that the acquisition of a new skill compels the child to master that skill and use it to achieve other skills. Until your infant is able to crawl, she is a passive observer of the world around her and mostly dependent upon other people for stimulation and pleasure. Walking opens up new horizons for her and gives her an insatiable appetite to explore and uncover the secrets of the wide world. She sees that doors are to be opened, drawers pulled out, buttons pushed, knobs turned, and objects taken apart. She is a going concern from dawn till dusk, stopping briefly to refuel on food and love, only to jump down again and continue her independent research of the world around her. She succumbs to an occasional nap and does not yield to the enemy of sleep without a fight.

Your little navigator does not chart her course carefully. A toddler's explorations are directed more by impulse and trial and error than by calculation and reasoning. Toddlers are not willfully destructive or disobedient. They simply have not developed control systems to govern their intense impulses. The late Selma Fraiberg stated beautifully in her book *The Magic Years*, "Toddlers exhibit a declaration of independence but they have no intentions of unseating the government."

The second year is often presented in very negative terms. Some mothers say, "The terrible twos—I'll be glad when this stage is over." Any self-respecting toddler would disagree with these unfair words and would feel that he is simply misunderstood. The media have done toddlers a disservice. If all children really acted in the way they are portrayed, there would be many "only children." For parents, this is one of the most exciting yet admittedly exhausting stages of child development. Your toddler is really not a negative little person, he is very positive. He knows absolutely what he wants, and he is determined to get it at all costs. The no-nos come from his outside world. Perhaps this should be called the "negative stage of parenting" rather than the negative stage of the child.

Toward the end of the second year the development of language gives the toddler another avenue of communication with the world around him. The combination of language and locomotion gives the toddler a newly found power to use the world around him for his own needs or desires. For example, being unable to get the right peg in the right hole, our frustrated toddler runs over and tugs on Mommy's skirt, saying, "Mommy do it." When a child begins to use another person as a resource for a problem he cannot solve by himself, he has learned a vital educational skill. The toddler also will vacillate between "I do it myself" and

"Mommy do it" followed by an incessant chain of "No!" and "Pick me up." This normal toddler behavior should not be interpreted as manipulation, which needs restricting, but rather as healthy communication, which needs an appropriate response. If you respond to a toddler's cues appropriately and with direction, he is motivated to develop further his newly discovered powers. If this motivation is directed rather than restrained, the toddler feels right, he is further stimulated to continue developing these powers, and his self-esteem prospers.

The dilemma between disciplining and directing a toddler is arriving at a proper balance, exerting just the right amount of guidance and restraint without hampering the toddler's desire to learn. Rather than regard this stage as a permanent threat to your parental powers, consider it a passing developmental stage.

Now that you are more familiar with usual and normal toddler behavior, learn how you can guide and direct, or discipline, that behavior into desirable avenues. (See the Bibliography for books about normal childhood behavior.)

Be available on an as-needed basis. Your toddler needs your support while he works out the anxiety that is created by his internal ambivalence. You are still the pivotal point in his widening universe. As he makes his daily rounds throughout the house, he periodically checks on your whereabouts, and he is comforted knowing you are there.

Be observant of your toddler's behavior. Watch for his cues that he needs you, but also be willing to accept his need for his own space. Part of achieving parental maturity and becoming an effective disciplinarian is having your radar system so finely tuned into your child that you pick up his signals on your screen and store each bit of information. A child who has a consistently available and observant caregiver intuitively feels that someone he loves is in tune with him. Consider for a moment your relationship with your heavenly Father; what a feeling of strength and security to know that He is available and observant of your behavior and of your needs.

Consider Your Child's Environment

Respect your toddler's healthy curiosity by moving your valuable and breakable family heirlooms up a few feet. Bring them down in a few years when she is old enough to reason with. The out-of-reach and out-of-sight environment is certainly much easier on child and parent than a constant stream of "no-no" or "don't touch." Constantly saying no and frustrating the natural drive to explore only serves to produce anger in your child on a continuous basis. The toddler-on-the-loose precautions are certainly safer and less exhausting than a system that requires the ever-watchful eyes of a protective mother.

Also, consider size-related needs by giving your child child-size furniture. Having her own small table and chairs in a corner of your kitchen (where the action is) allows a young child to be comfortable sitting for a longer time, thus encouraging task completion and concentration. Since it is normal and healthy behavior for her to turn knobs, push buttons, and pull drawers, give your child her own things to turn, push, and pull. A curious toddler deserves at least one eye-level drawer in the kitchen that she can pull out, sort through, and fill with her own belongings. Place safety latches on cupboards that are off limits. Encouraging her to get into her own things will cause her to be less interested in the things she should not have.

Encourage hands-on learning. Give your toddler things to carry, blocks to stack, things to pour, wagons to pull, safe places to climb, and objects to touch. A child's hands are tools she can use to explore and learn cause-and-effect relationships. For this reason, sensitive childhood development experts recommend that you do no hand slapping to discourage her touching things. Hand slapping to a curious toddler just beginning to reach out into the world is probably just as insulting as face slapping is to an adult. The more positive feedback she receives ("Thank you for bringing Mommy the clothes"; "Show me your car"), the less likely she is to want to touch the things that are off limits. (The concept of "me" and "mine" is important at this age too.) Create a positive environment, a get-into-things and a hands-on approach that respects the normal, innate curiosity of a developing toddler and makes negative discipline less necessary.

Take a few minutes here to dwell upon one basic goal of discipline, and that is to create an environment that does not create a conflict of wills. Creating a child-considered environment contributes to your maturity as parents who sincerely want to discipline your child. Learn to respect your child's different need levels at different stages of development. Rather than viewing discipline as a parental obligation to suppress your child until he is old enough to act like an adult, let your child act like a child so he can feel like a child. If you view discipline as guidance, you will regard a child-considered environment as guiding or disciplining your home environment so that the environment itself may discipline the child.

Be creative in high-risk situations that make discipline difficult. It is unrealistic to expect a curious toddler to walk down the aisle in a supermarket and not touch anything. I would be very suspicious of a young child who walked like an obedient soldier with his arms at his sides down the aisle of a supermarket and did not try to grab all those delightful things just begging to be grabbed. Keep his arms and hands full of things so he is completely "grabbed up." Let him help you grab things. After all, that is the model he sees—his mother is walking down the aisle grabbing things. Or keep him safely seated in the shopping cart (with a restraint strap) and carry on a conversation with him that lets him feel included in the shopping.

Replace "no-no" with "yes-yes" or simply "stop." One of the first words an infant says is *no* because *no* is one of the first words he hears. When an eighteen month old is sitting quietly and playing, nobody says anything to him. But let him start exploring and he excites everybody; he gets lots of attention. The child does not know intuitively, in most instances, which behavior is right or wrong, but he soon learns which behavior gets the quickest response from adults. And he learns behavior directly from the behavior you use toward him. Speak politely and gently even when correcting him, even though it is hard not to sound rude when you are irritated. And rather than grabbing a "no-no" from his hands, model asking for it ("Give it to Momma, please") and show him how to place it in your hand for you. If the object is dangerous, grabbing it may actually inflict injury. You can restrain his hand so that the scissors (or whatever) cannot do any damage while you are teaching him to hand it to you. These are matters of common courtesy—the way you would respect a friend. Behavior modification principles are especially applicable to a two year old who will naturally gravitate toward the behavior that gets him the most response (positive or negative). If a child likes the response he gets from good behavior, he will be inclined to repeat this behavior. Acknowledge him or catch him in the act of being good. Simply use more affirmative words in talking with your toddler and fewer negative words. If he is zeroing in on your valuable vase, rather than descend on him from above with an almighty "no-no," gently but firmly redirect his probing hands toward a safer object and quickly rescue the vase to higher ground.

Adopt the "why" principle. When your young child apparently misbehaves, train yourself to ask yourself, *Why is he doing that?* Is he tired, bored, hungry, or sick? Is he simply trying to get attention? Is he engaging in a power struggle? Is he trying to fit into a group but has not found his role? If you first approach your child's behavior by asking *why* he is doing something, rather than asking *what* he is doing, you will focus first on the child and second on the act. It is in such instances that knowing your child begins to pay off. In so doing you will understand better the feelings behind the child's behavior and be able to take effective steps to channel his behavior.

A good example of this in our family is our sixteen-month-old daughter. She playfully and gleefully begins to hit (aggressively touch) her mother on the head or face. Her mother expresses displeasure and asks her to "stop." Usually she doesn't, unless her mother picks her up and changes the situation. She is having fun and doesn't understand that it hurts. So her mother gives her something more appropriate to hit; she holds out her hand and says, "Gimme five." The hitting continues with great gusto, and both parties in the game enjoy it. Focusing on the why is good parental training for disciplining the older child when it is often necessary to focus primarily on the child's feelings rather than the action. (Don't ask your older child, "Why are you doing this?" but, "What are you doing?" It helps his ability to evaluate his behavior correctly if he can state *what* he is doing.)

Between twelve and eighteen months of age most conflicts occur between the child and his environment rather than between the parent and his child. Therefore, most of your authority and discipline are directed toward taking charge of your child's environment and thus indirectly setting limits for him. Even before your toddler has begun walking, you have covered electric outlets, locked your cupboards, removed breakable objects, covered sharp table corners, removed small objects that can be swallowed. Taking charge of a child's environment is an important part of disciplining him. A toddler's internal discipline operates at a very simple level. His behavior is directed toward what makes him feel good and away from what makes him not feel good. For example, a hand on a hot stove is not likely to be repeated, but a hand in a cookie jar is very likely to be repeated.

Toward the end of their second year together (eighteen months to two years), a parent's role shifts somewhat from environmental designer to educator and authority figure. The child's level of dependence is still high, and he is still quite ambivalent. However, at the end of the second year his behavior is usually directed less by impulse and trial and error and more by thinking and calculating. By this time he has learned cause-and-effect and how to manipulate his environment to get what he needs. For example, he begins to think of a footstool as the great equalizer to make him taller. He also knows that the cookies are in the cupboard. He puts the two together, figuring out that if he pulls the stool in front of the cupboard he can climb up and get the cookies.

The ability to calculate coupled with somewhat impulsive behavior usually leads to some power struggles between parent and child at this age. And this is where parents emerge as authority figures. A child must know who is in charge of his environment; the younger he is when he learns and feels who is in charge, the less traumatic this power struggle is to both parent and child. At this point let me impress upon you a very important consideration in disciplining your child: a child wants and needs limits. A child needs security and direction and becomes confused when he is without controls. Psalm 23:4 says, "Your rod and Your staff, they comfort me."

■ Set Limits and Provide Structure

In the past decade a lot of New Age psychology has crept into the field of Christian discipline, resulting in the parents taking on the role of amateur psychologists, negotiators, and diplomats, rather than authority figures.

Parents worry that they must always be psychologically correct in talking to their child, so they tend to be wimpy and overpermissive. Children need limits. In our family of eight children, we have learned that our kids wouldn't thrive and we would not survive without limits.

A key to discipline is setting limits and providing structure. Structure means setting the conditions that encourage desirable behavior to happen. For example, you set limits in your home by teaching the child that there are yes-touches and no-touches throughout his environment (for that matter, throughout his whole life). That's the limit-setting part of discipline.

Yet that is not enough. Structure means setting the conditions that make these limits easier to enforce or setting the child up to behave. So you don't have to go through a shopping nightmare of constantly saying no to your curious toddler, don't take him shopping at four in the afternoon when he is tired and hungry. You structure your shopping trip at a time of the day when his behavior is usually best. It's not enough to set limits by constantly saying no to the toddler as he explores all the curious objects throughout the house. You structure his explorations by providing a childproof and child-considered environment for busy minds and busy bodies to play. ■

Develop Your Role as an Authority Figure

"No, no, no!" is a common parental outburst around the end of the first year, making parents cognizant of their emerging role as authority figures. Your role is an authority figure, taking charge of your child's environment. By creating a child-considered environment, you encourage your child's natural developmental curiosities to flourish while you protect her from harm until she has the wisdom and discernment to know her limits. Throughout Scripture are clear mandates to parents to take charge of their children (Prov. 19:18, 22:6; Eph. 6:4).

Authority does not mean that suddenly when she is two years old you decide to clamp down on your child. If you have laid the foundation of discipline in the first year, if you have fulfilled the conditions of attachment parenting, your role as authority figure will naturally evolve. The earliest condition that helps your role of authority figure evolve is you attitude of openness to your child's cues. Being open to your baby's cues and becoming "giving" parents do not mean you are losing control.

The first few years of parenting are similar to Christ's ministry. Jesus was clearly in charge of His disciples. He was a strong authority figure to them, but He was, first of all, a servant to them. He washed their feet (John 13:5).

Parents who use restraint early and try to rear their children according to their preconceived ideas of how children *ought* to be (rather than how their individual children really are) are candidates for becoming ineffective authority figures later on. In my practice, I actually look for the cues of openness in parents during the first few months of their babies' lives so that I can counsel them more effectively about discipline.

Parents have a God-given right to expect obedience from their children. God's order for children is that they obey their parents: "Children, obey your parents in all things, for this is well pleasing to the Lord" (Col. 3:20). The biblical basis for authority is not only obedience but also respect for authority. "Honor your father and your mother," the commandment says. The term *honor* implies obedience plus respect. It is honor that you want from your children, not just obedience. Although obedience is owed to you, respect for authority is not an unconditional right of parents; it must be earned. The attachment styles of parenting will help you earn this honor.

Some parents may think that through the use of the *rod* (which they interpret to mean spanking), they can force their children to do what they want them to do, that is, to obey. However, the biblical basis for the word *obey* does not mean simply "to do as I say." It means "to hear intelligently," from the Hebrew root word *shama*. This implies that children need to be old enough and mature enough to understand what they are hearing their parents ask or command. It is difficult for parents to know how much their toddlers really understand. Most toddlers understand much more than they say because receptive language development is more advanced than expressive language. They understand the words for concrete objects they can recognize, such as *doggie, horsey, cat,* and so on. But they usually cannot understand abstract concepts or attitudes. They can say, "No, no" (it's easy to say and they hear it often enough), but they cannot understand how and why they are expected to obey. When they say "No" they don't mean "No, I *won't*" they mean "No, I *don't want* to." It is your job as parents to help them "want to" obey. This is known as motivating your child—it sets the stage for inner-directed discipline later on.

■ Turning an Accident into an Opportunity

In our family of eight we naturally have had to clean up many puddles of spilled milk. One day

our three year old, Lauren, was opening the refrigerator door and out spilled a carton of milk
all over the floor. I was late for work and this
mess occurred at an inconvenient time. Before I
could get angry, Martha intervened.

She knelt down next to Lauren, gave her eye-
to-eye contact and a supporting hand on her
shoulder, and Lauren willingly helped Martha
clean up the mess. I asked Martha how she kept
from getting angry. She said, "I asked myself if I
were Lauren, how would I want my mother to
act in this situation?"

Martha illustrated an important part of discipline: getting behind the eyes of your child and
responding accordingly. Kids make inconvenient
mistakes, and many of these are beyond parental
control, but you can control your reactions to
these accidents. In many discipline situations, accidents provide an opportunity for improving
your parent-child relationship. █

Toddlers may be incapable of completely fulfilling
the biblical meaning of obedience, which is why spanking them before they are old enough to understand
why they are being spanked would not be in keeping
with the true biblical concept of obedience. Toddlers
can be trained that a certain action warrants a certain
response; this is negative training. Positive training uses
all the steps of attachment parenting and the creatively
designed child-considered environment to elicit the
same response. For example you want your twenty-
month-old to come get in the car to go shopping.
You see he is busy with his trucks and will hate being
interrupted. Instead of just telling him to come, you

motivate him by talking about something fun you'll do when you get there (see the doggies, ride the horsey). How much nicer for both of you than for you to have to pick up a kicking, screaming child and force him into his car seat.

Another example of positive training is to help a child leave an activity that he is enjoying when you have a time constraint. First, try to give him a five-minute warning so he doesn't have to cope with a sudden shift. Then if he is upset with having to leave his play, help him say, "Bye-bye trucks, see you later." Bringing closure to his play gives him a sense of control when he can say good-bye and look forward to a re-union. Parents who truly know their children will be able to choose which approach is in accordance with God's design for disciplining their individual children.

A child's parents can whip him into obedience, but they only can love him into developing an attitude of respect for them. *The American Heritage Dictionary* defines *respect:* "to feel or show esteem for; to honor." The couple who has practiced attachment parenting has earned their child's trust; they are appreciated as the source of his feelings of rightness. That child considers his parents worthy of esteem. It is imperative that a child respect his parents because this provides a basis for his attitude toward his adult world in general and toward any authority figure in particular. The more a child respects his parents' authority, the more readily he will respect God's commandments. If your child does not respect reasonable authority, you have a real problem that can have far-reaching consequences. The best way to teach respect toward parents is for parents to respect their child as a person.

Disciplining the Child
Two to Three Years Old

The main elements of discipline in a toddler have been discussed: (1) your child becomes secure in her trust relationship with you and therefore feels right within herself; (2) you are in harmony with your child and really know her; (3) you have designed her environment appropriately to respect her curiosity yet protect her from harm; and (4) you have planted the seeds to help you become effective authority figures.

The two to three year old is characterized by three interesting features: (1) mastery of expressive language; (2) increasing awareness of self; and (3) the beginning of social peer relationships. The two year old is learning to verbalize his feelings and demands, which enables him to hold the attention of adults and of his peers. He shows less tendency to act out his anxiety because he is able to express it with words. His developing language skills enable him to become a truly social person and enable him to manipulate (there is a positive aspect to this) his adult environment. This ability adds "bigness" to his concept of self.

A child's increasing ability to walk and talk her way into what she wants or feels she needs (the difference between a want and a need is as confusing to the child as it is to the parent at this stage) is a tremendous boost to her emerging but still fragile self-esteem. Bearing this in mind, you can effectively discipline your two year old. First, by recognizing that two year olds are driven to use their limited abilities to manipulate their environments and to improve their end of the parent/child communication network and, second, by responding appropriately to these drives for communication. An *appropriate* response is emphasized because this implies achieving a balance between responding in a way that further motivates her desire to improve her communication and increase her self-esteem, and responding in a way that is governed by reasonable restraint on what and how much she gets. This is the principle of *delayed gratification*, which is so vitally important in discipline of the child at any age. (How to teach your child delayed gratification effectively is an important point discussed later.)

The development of a disciplined child is a continuum: how you discipline your child at one stage of development will carry over into the effectiveness of the next stage of development. If you have succeeded in setting appropriate limits and if you have seen outside control in your almost two year old, he will begin to show some inner controls of his own during the next year. By the time your child is two years old he can begin to show some inner control and become more certain of his limits because he has had the previous year to sort them out.

At this stage, stubbornness will occasionally rear its head (in some children more than in others), but there is generally less negativism on both sides. Most two year olds will become less clingy and obstinate, and at the same time, their parents become less restraining. By two years of age, most children have suffered enough bumps and bruises to have learned the limits of their home environments and therefore feel more comfortable and secure and in control of their own bodies. The behavior of the two year old becomes less impulsive, and he considers alternatives before acting. He has become increasingly aware of cause-and-effect relationships. The usual two year old is very egocentric. He sees things entirely from his own point of view, and he tries to figure out how he can use the outside world to suit his own needs. Appreciate this as normal behavior at this age, a behavior that is not to be squelched but directed.

Since being egocentric and using expressive language to manipulate his environment is normal behavior for a two to three year old, look now at what is appropriate parental response to this God-given behavior. First, the term *manipulation*, which unfortunately has fallen into disrepute, needs to be clarified. It has come to mean a method whereby a child wraps her parents around her little finger and dangles them as puppets in her exciting world of unending sensual (meaning the five senses) delights. "I don't want to feel manipulated" is a common parental feeling at this stage, which often leads you to overreact and misinterpret your children's behavior.

At this stage of a child's development there is healthy manipulation and unhealthy manipulation. A child sees her activities mainly as communication, not manipulation. A young child with a healthy self-esteem who feels good using all her primitive tools to communicate with her environment (people and things) will normally try to get everything she can to fulfill totally her insatiable appetite for pleasure. A two year old does not yet have enough inner control of what and how much of any good thing is best for her, and that is why she needs direction. Parents, avoid the tendency to overreact to the feeling, "I'm not going to let her manipulate me." This usually results in a power struggle in which your primary communication with your child will be negative (what you are not going to let her do) rather than positive (what you are going to let her do or have). When you direct her manipulation, she is encouraged to communicate her needs, and she feels right in communicating them. Put very simply, a child should always feel right in "asking and seeking and knocking." She should always feel that there is a tuned-in receiver for the signals she sends out. It is then up to you, striving for effective Christian discipline, to receive all of these signals and feed back to your child what, in your judgment, she should have and what she should not have. Let's call this "selective gratification." Here is where you begin planting the seed for one of the most important elements of effective discipline, which peaks in the middle childhood and teenage period, and that is the concept of delayed gratification.

Unhealthy manipulation occurs when a parent, by being unavailable, unobservant, or uninterested, either ignores the child's signals and feeds back nothing to him or receives all of the child's signals and does not selectively process them, thus becoming overindulgent in giving the child everything he wants. Both extremes—the child who receives nothing and the child who receives everything—are equally unhealthy.

How do you develop selective gratification of your child's demands? Follow all the principles: be available; be observant; know your child and the direction he should go; and, above all, pray, asking God for wisdom.

In addition to verbal language, body language is extremely important at this stage. Two year olds are very affectionate; this is the stage of open arms and "pick me up." Become a hugs-and-kisses family. The ability to give and receive affection is one of the most important behavior-improving influences in disciplining a child.

Encourage Good Behavior

Acknowledge your child's creativity. Two year olds show varying desires and abilities to be creative. The skills of scribbling, stacking, finger painting, and modeling with clay are beginning at this stage. Your little architect takes great pride in her creative accomplishments and is eager to share them with you. No matter how haphazard it may seem to you, to her the page full of scribble is an artistic accomplishment, and she wants an approving response from her most trusted art critic. A positive response to your child's creative accomplishments at this stage becomes one of the most powerful reinforcers of positive behavior. If a child feels better from the response she gets from putting things together, rather than from tearing them apart, she is likely to continue the desirable behavior.

Maintain order in the house. Between two and three years of age, children show an innate appreciation for order. A young child's developing brain is searching for organization, and this starts with organizing his belongings. Your role as designer of your child's environment increases to organizer of his environment.

These specific suggestions will help you provide order in your child's environment and use this order as a powerful enforcer of desirable behavior.

1. Instead of piling toys in toy boxes and corners, use low shelves with one-foot-square compartments, each containing one or two valued toys. Too many toys in places that are too small confuse the child who is already trying to sort out all the clutter in the busy world around him.

2. Give your child his own table and chairs. Child-size furniture improves his comfort and his attention span.

3. Use eye-level wooden pegs where he can hang his clothing.

This orderly environment complements the child's orderly mind and also encourages a sense of responsibility. One of the most common difficulties I see in children of all ages is the lack of an inner sense of responsibility. The development of a child's responsibility for his own actions begins with a sense of responsibility for his own belongings, and this should begin around two years of age.

Provide good nutrition. It may seem unusual to talk about good nutrition in regard to childhood discipline. However, you are on the offensive. Discipline is still being considered in the positive sense—what you can do to encourage desirable behavior. Good nutrition (or the lack of it) can have a profound effect on behavior. I recommend three feeding practices that may improve your child's behavior and therefore may contribute positively to your discipline relationship.

First, *breastfeed* your infant as long as both members of the nursing couple enjoy the relationship. I encourage mothers to think of breastfeeding in terms of years and not months. At this point you may ask, "What on earth has this to do with disciplining my child?" Early in this chapter on discipline you read about the importance of the young infant's developing a secure attachment and trust in his caregiver as a prerequisite for that caregiver's becoming an effective authority figure later on. Breastfeeding mothers simply spend more time with their children. Breast-fed infants eat more often, and they spend more time in their mothers' arms and derive more skin-to-skin and eye-to-eye contact. I am not saying that breastfeeding mothers love their children any more than bottlefeeding mothers, but I do feel that breastfeeding gives the mother a head start in knowing her child better, and the child is given a head start in feeling right. These two elements are basic to the foundation for effective discipline.

The second feeding practice I encourage you to consider is *nibbling*. This may sound like heresy, a blatant attempt to undermine the accepted custom of requiring a young child to sit still, consume three square meals a day, and eat nothing between meals. But consider the limitations of the young child, especially at two or three years of age. He does not have the attention span to sit still and finish a large meal. He is simply too busy. This often results in mealtimes becoming battles between parents and child instead of positive experiences. Medically speaking, it is better for a young child to nibble on nutritious foods all day long because he avoids frequent blood-sugar swings and the mood changes that often accompany them in an active child. This is why the behavior of young children deteriorates in late morning and mid-afternoon when they are the most hungry and their blood sugar is the lowest. See chapter 6 of *Now That Baby Is Home* for tips on feeding your toddler and young child.

The third practice that will improve your child's behavior is *avoiding junk food*. (See related nutrition information, "Breakfast for a Growing Brain," p. 203.)

Give Spiritual Training

Parents often ask, "At what stage of my child's development do I introduce the concept of God into discipline?" It is much easier to bring God into discipline at this stage if you have brought Him into your lives very early in your marriage. The pathway to successful Christian parenting is a series of personal relationships.

The first relationship is between you and God, by committing yourselves to follow His commandments and by acknowledging Jesus as your personal Savior and Lord. The second relationship is a dual commitment: you commit yourself to your spouse and to a lifelong Christian marriage, and you commit this relationship to God. You acknowledge Him as the supreme marriage counselor from whom you will receive the necessary strength and wisdom to grow in a fulfilled Christian marriage. After you have committed yourselves to God as a couple, your next relationship is to commit yourselves to Him as parents. From the moment of conception, pray daily over your preborn child, acknowledging God as the architect and protector of your developing fetus. After birth, pray daily for your baby, asking God for wisdom to rear him or her according to His plan. Daily read God's Word aloud to your baby from his very early days. At around fifteen to eighteen months show him pictures and talk about Jesus. His own picture Bible would be a good way to start.

If you have brought God into your lives early in these relationships, you have laid a foundation for naturally imparting the concept of God to your child when he is two years of age. Without this foundation you will be less comfortable talking with your child about God because you do not know God's working in your own lives. It goes back to the basic principle that you cannot give to your children what you do not have.

How to Teach Your Two Year Old About God

Here are specific examples as to how you as Christian parents can introduce God to your child.

1. *Pray for your child.* Thank God for your child every day. Ask God to watch over your child's development and to give you wisdom in rearing him in the way he should go. By the time your child is two years old, a spiritual feeding of daily prayer becomes as natural a part of child care as food for the body does.

From the day of the birth of our fifth child, each night before retiring I would lay my hands on my little daughter and spend a few moments in prayer. A few nights I went to sleep having forgotten to do this, but I would soon awaken with the feeling that as I lay down to sleep, I had forgotten to lay someone else down to sleep. I then performed my duty as spiritual leader of my home and put my hands on my little daughter, thanking God for the blessings of her day and asking Him to be with her during the night. I then retired with a comfortable feeling that we both would sleep better, because in the quiet of the night Someone who never goes off call is watching over us.

Daily prayer is vital to Christian family discipline. It becomes a discipline, a persistent spiritual habit by which the parent continuously prays, "Father, I invite You into our family; You are a trusted and vital family member (head of the family, in fact), and my day is not complete unless we talk to each other." By the time your child is two years old, she hears the words *God* and *Jesus* spoken in association with love and protection so that by the time she is three years old, she feels God's presence. A child's concept of God is very simplistic, and it is probably limited to a feeling: "Mom and Dad talk about Him all the time, He must be a very important person; He loves me, He is a big Person." Such primitive concepts are vital to laying the foundation of the child's regard for God as the authority figure at a later age. One of the characteristics of toddlers' language skills is that they receive and understand much more than they say. They probably will understand more of the concept of God if they have been saturated with hearing about God from birth (Deut. 6:6–9).

One Christian mother confided in me that she feels her two year old knows Jesus. She had been praying with her child every night from the time he was one year old. When he was two the mother walked by her child's bedroom shortly after praying him to sleep and heard him saying, "Jesus . . . Amen." What went on in that two year old's absorbent mind in the few moments between "Jesus" and "Amen" only the child feels and God knows.

2. *Sing with your infant.* Between the ages of one and two, babies can mimic the gestures of songs. For example, as early as nine months, our daughter Erin lifted up her arms at the cue of "praise Jesus." Following our evening meal prayer we have a custom of singing the following song.

> *Let's just praise the Lord, praise the Lord;*
> *Let's just lift our hands to heaven and praise the Lord.*
> *(Repeat, all the time lifting up your hands.)*

Initially, Erin would simply watch this family praise. Eventually, she began raising her hands when we did. By fifteen months, as soon as the mealtime grace was finished, in anticipation of the praise song to follow she would raise her hands right on cue (sometimes reminding us to sing). Praising the Lord was being imprinted upon her heart even before she could grasp intellectually the real meaning of what was being sung. As we all joined hands, bowed our heads, and became quiet for prayer, she did the same. At seventeen months she was able to remind us to say the blessing by reaching for my hand on one side and her mother's hand on the other side. She knows we are supposed to do something special before we eat. Babies can sense praise to God long before they really understand it.

3. *Read to your child about God.* Two year olds (and even younger children) have a fascination for books. A Bible picture book and a loving parent's arm are a winning combination for holding his attention. Two year olds are able to understand the simple Bible picture books about Jesus. By reading to your child and showing him pictures about the life of Jesus, you are teaching him a vital message. He learns: "A Man in my picture book does all kinds of nice things, and my mommy and daddy talk about this same Man all the time. He must be a special Person." If you can convey to your two year old that one message, that Jesus is a special Person, you have done most of your job for laying the foundation for his deeper understanding of Christ and God in subsequent stages. In Deuteronomy 6:6 God said, "These words which I command you today shall be in your heart."

Discipline Undesirable Behavior

You should now know how to encourage desirable behavior in your young child as the basis for effective discipline. This should be your primary focus and consume the majority of your energy in disciplining your child. However, as Proverbs 22:15 says, "Foolishness is bound up in the heart of a child." Your child will get off the track at some time. There is in every child this bent toward disobedience and undesirable behavior. You don't have to teach them to disobey. To this reality God added, "But the rod of correction will drive it far from him." In this mandate, God has told parents very simply but very clearly, "Parents, take charge of your child; pick him up and get him back on the track; no matter what it takes to do the job, do it." (Please see Chapter 6, pages 146–150, for further explanations of the "rod" verses.)

In discussing how to correct your young child's misbehavior, you need to understand an important point. Some children by their inherent nature have more foolishness than others. Some children take longer to get the point than others. There is an undesirable part of every child's temperament that God has allowed to be there from the moment of birth. We cannot reverse it. We can only modify it and channel it. Parents, do not look back and feel guilty and wonder where you have gone wrong. If you have been blessed with a high-need child who is endowed with a greater than average amount of foolishness, accept this and get on with realizing that your God-given role is to impart to your child above-average discipline.

Before discussing specific examples, there are general principles to consider in nearly all situations of correcting your child. The first principle is to recognize the vital ingredients of a strong foundation on which discipline by correction is based. A child must feel right within himself, and he must be secure in his trust and love relationship with his primary caregivers, usually his parents.

Based upon these fundamental feelings within the child, the second principle is that in every action toward disciplinary correction you want to convey two feelings to your child. (1) "I love you, my son or my daughter. You are very valuable to me and to God. You are a special person." (2) "Because I love you and because I am in charge, I will remain in charge until you are able to take full responsibility for your own actions."

The third principle is a simple concept of behavior modification, the principle of reinforcement. This means that behavior that is rewarded will continue and behavior that is not rewarded will not continue. Behavior that makes a child feel good will continue and behavior that makes a child feel bad will not.

The final principle in correcting your child is to pray and seek counsel if your disciplinary methods are not comfortable and are not working. If you base your disciplinary actions on the above considerations, you are not likely to go wrong.

There are several common undesirable behaviors in a two to three year old.

1. *Whining.* Language is a newly found power for a young child, and it is only normal that he will use his God-given power to get what he wants. A young child quickly learns what kind of communication gets the quickest reaction from his parents. It is important that you are able to say so nicely, "I'm sorry I can't give you more." There is nothing to be gained by being rude in words or tone of voice or gesture. Not getting a cookie will cause him to feel angry—don't provoke him to more anger yourself. "Fathers, do not provoke your children to wrath" (Eph. 6:4). Take the example of the usual cookie jar struggle. Your two year old has already consumed his allotted number of cookies for the day.

He has already been told, "No more." He decides to test the limits and ask for one more. His initial opener is usually a feeble whining gesture toward the cookie jar. When your child opens his communication with a whine, it is usually a clue that he is uncertain of the response he is going to get. He really feels he is not going to get what he wants and probably shouldn't get what he wants. The whining child gets the anticipated negative response: request denied. Not willing to give up without a fight, his whining increases in loudness, hoping that you will give in to him just to get him off your back and out of your ears. At this point you may say: "Billy [address your child by name, because this raises his status as a person], Mommy knows that you want a cookie [you understand his position]. You have already had three cookies today, and I'm sorry, but I am not going to give you any more [he has been treated fairly, at least according to your rules, or for the older child, according to a mutually agreed-upon allotment]. My ears will not listen to whining [or God did not make Mommy's ears to listen to whining; the undesirable behavior is not rewarded]. Now come over and talk nicely to Mommy and help me slice these apples, and we can have some together after suppertime [desirable behavior is acknowledged and rewarded and delayed gratification is encouraged]."

If the whining is mild, not too irritating, and diminishing in degree, you simply may ignore this undesirable behavior since you said your ears do not listen to it anyway and the fire seems to be dying out (undesirable behavior unrewarded will stop). However, suppose Billy continues his increasingly irritating whining. Sit down next to him, put your hand lovingly on his shoulder, look him squarely in the eyes, and say, "I'm sorry,

Billy, that I can't give you any more cookies. Now I'm going to set the timer for one minute. When the buzzer goes off, I expect you to start talking nicely with Mommy. Then we will have some fun. And if you do not, you will go to your room." You have conveyed expected behavior, given him a little time and space to sort it out, and conveyed the consequences of continued undesirable behavior, which he is free to choose or not to choose. If at this point Billy stops whining, it is very important to follow through with the reward for desirable behavior and sit down and have some fun with him. He learns that it is more desirable to work with the family government than to overthrow it. Your sitting with him may be just what he needed.

Suppose the buzzer goes off, and Billy is still whining. More than the cookie is on the line in this illustration: your child's feelings are out of control and your authority is on the line If you give in to your child simply to get him off your back or take the path of least resistance, you are out of God's will as a parent. You are also perpetuating this undesirable behavior and generally weakening your future stand when confrontations of higher priority than the cookie are at stake.

By three years of age your child should be able to comprehend most of a meaningful dialogue: "Billy, God gave you a beautiful voice that Mommy likes to hear. He doesn't want you to whine, and I don't want you to whine. Let's both kneel down and ask God to help you talk nicely to Mommy and not whine. Come, let's do this together." You turn a potentially negative disciplinary situation into a positive one. You have made your point and cleared the air of ill feelings. You also have gone one step further; you have conveyed to your child that there exists a support Person whom you value and whom you want him to value and that prayer is a valuable resource in times of need.

2. *Temper tantrums.* Two basic inner feelings in your child prompt most temper tantrums. First, a two year old has an intense desire to perform and act, but often the desire is greater than the capability. Facing this reality may lead to intense frustration that is released in a healthy, outward tantrum. This kind of tantrum needs loving support, gentleness, and understanding; guide the child toward successfully achieving the activity or channel her direction into a more easily achievable activity suited to her personality and achievement level.

The second cause of temper tantrums is hearing no just when the two year old's newly found power and desire for "bigness" propel her toward a certain act. Accepting an outside force contrary to her strong will is a difficult conflict she cannot handle without a fight. She wants to be big, but her world tells her and shows her how small she is. She is upset, but she does not have the ability to handle conflicting emotions with reason, so she copes with her inner emotions by a display of outward emotions, which are termed a *tantrum*. Think of your child's tantrums in terms of her newly forming sense of self and inner control becoming unglued. She needs someone to keep her from falling apart.

The most frightening temper tantrums are breath-holding spells. During the rage of a tantrum a child may hold her breath, turn blue, become limp, and may even faint. Breath-holding spells resemble convulsions; they cause the tantrum to become even more alarming to the already worried parents. Fortunately, most children who hold their breath resume normal breathing just as they are on the brink of passing out. Even those children who faint momentarily quickly resume normal breathing before harming themselves. These episodes usually stop when the child is old enough to express his anger verbally.

Temper tantrums can be exhausting and frightening experiences for both child and parent. Discipline mild tantrums just as you would discipline whining. In the more severe temper tantrums the child is out of control, and he is confused about how to regain control, even if he wants to.

How are temper tantrums handled? First, realize that you can't handle them; you only support your child when he has them. Temper tantrums reflect your child's emotions which *he* has to handle. Excessive interference deprives the child of the mechanism of releasing his inner tensions, but too little support leaves him to cope all by himself without the strength to do so effectively. What is the issue causing the temper tantrum? If he has chosen an impossible task and it becomes apparent he is not going to achieve it but won't give up, simply be on standby. Temper tantrums bring out the best in intuitive mothering. Keep your arms extended and your attitude accepting. Often a few soothing words or a little help ("I'll untie the knot and you put on your shoe") will put him on the road to recovery.

If the issue at stake is a power struggle of wills (for example, she wants a toy that she should not have), then the temper tantrum should be approached with the usual firm and loving double whammy of effective discipline: "I love you, my child, and I am in charge here." Sometimes, a strong-willed child will lose complete control of himself during a tantrum. When her behavior reaches this stage, simply hold her very firmly but lovingly and explain: "You are angry and you have lost control [you understand her position]. I am holding you tightly because I love you, I want to help you, and you will be all right [I'm in charge here]." You may discover that after a minute of struggling to free herself, a rigid child melts into your arms as if thanking you for rescuing her. My wife, Martha, ended one of our little daughter's tantrums on a spiritual note with, "Now let's pray together."

Temper tantrums in public places are embarrassing, and it is often difficult to consider your child's feelings first. *What will people think of me as a mother?* is likely to be your first thought. In this situation, if it becomes uncomfortable for both of you, remove your child to another room where he can have his tantrum in private. If the tantrum is based upon an inner frustration, then open arms and an accepting attitude will help defuse the child's explosive behavior. If the issue is one of defiance, again your authority is at stake, and all the levels of discipline mentioned in the example of whining should be carried out. Sometimes a child who is crying uncontrollably can't stop when you ask him to. He may or may not want to stop, but he literally cannot get hold of himself. If he wants to stop, an offer to pray with him for help from God is all that is needed for both of you. An in-arms prayer time is extremely comforting.

Sometimes tantrums can be so exhausting to parents that giving into the child seems easier because he probably stops his disruptive behavior immediately.

However, keep in mind the principle that undesirable behavior, if rewarded, will persist. In addition to weakening your authority, rewarding temper tantrums will plant the seed in the child that aggressive and violent behavior will get him what he wants.

Tantrums often occur when parents impose unrealistic expectations on a child. Expecting a curious toddler to be a model of obedience in a toy store where he is surrounded by a smorgasbord of tempting delights may be asking too much. Children who are overly tired or hungry are especially prone to mood changes and temper tantrums, which may explain why many temper tantrums occur in the late morning or late afternoon when children are most tired and most hungry. Appropriately timed naps and the practice of nibbling may lessen the tendency for these tantrums.

Some tantrums occur when the child, during a high-need period, senses that her parents are not tuned in to her. She resorts to a tantrum in order to break through to them.

Most temper tantrums do not have lasting effects on the child. Fortunately, toddlers have a magnificent resilience for recovering from temper tantrums. They usually do not sulk for long periods of time, and a properly supported tantrum usually wears off quickly (but may leave parents worn out). Parents, take heart. The child's stage of temper tantrums seldom lasts long, and it is self-limiting for several reasons: his physical abilities eventually catch up with his desire for accomplishment; he does not like his inner feelings during a tantrum; and as soon as he develops enough language to express his emotions in words, his tantrum-like actions will mellow.

3. *Aggressive behavior against other children* (biting, hitting, scratching, pushing). There are as many theories about biting as there are teeth. Biting begins between the ages of eighteen months and two and a half years in a preverbal child and lessens when the child can communicate his feelings effectively with his tongue instead of his teeth. Because a toddler's mouth and hands are his first tools of communication, biting and hitting are to him forms of communication that are not intrinsically bad. The young child soon learns what is socially acceptable behavior by the response he gets from his victim or a nearby adult. If Isaac Newton had been a psychologist rather than a physicist, perhaps he would have worded his first law of child behavior: "For every undesirable action there is an equal and opposite reaction." The more quickly a young child can learn that undesirable behavior yields an undesirable response, the more quickly he will stop this behavior.

To stop a child's biting and hitting, consider these points. Determine the circumstances conducive to your child's biting, usually several children in a small space with a few toys. If your child shows aggressive activity with large groups in small spaces, your first disciplinary action is to design his environment and attempt to avoid circumstances that entice him to bite. In disciplining the biter, as with any undesirable behavior, consider first the feeling and the cause behind the action, rather than the action itself. Disciplining the biter is good training for you to think first why he is doing something rather than what he is doing. If considering the feelings within your child is your first step from which to proceed toward further disciplinary action, it is likely that your entire method of discipline will be more successful. Success is determined if the action stops and the child gains a learning experience.

Beware of falling into the trap of negatively reinforcing the biter. Biting attracts attention very quickly. If the child wants to be the instant center of attention, biting is sure to bring everybody running and set him apart as a special person. In some instances biting fulfills the craving in some children for attention, which reinforces their undesirable behavior. I feel that these attention-getting behaviors occur in a small percentage of biters and in these cases the "ignore it" advice may be applicable.

In general, however, do not ignore undesirable behavior in which one child harms another. Biting is not only hard on the tender little arms of unsuspecting victims, but it is also hard on parents. The parent of the biter is both disturbed and embarrassed, and the parent of the bitee is naturally upset that her child has been hurt. Negative feelings between parents may result. You can ease a potentially tense situation by discussing beforehand with the other parent that your child is a biter and that you are aware of his need for supervision. Biters always should be carefully supervised in groups. When a child bites, immediately remove him from the play group with appropriate admonitions such as, "Biting hurts, it is wrong, and you will sit in the corner or stay in this room until . . ." This isolation will teach the biter a valuable social lesson.

"Should I bite him back?" is certainly a valid question that a parent of a persistent biter may ask. No! Don't bite him back. Biting is an immature act, and you are a mature person. Therefore I am uncomfortable with the role modeling of a parent's biting a child.

■ Breaking the Biting Habit

Keep biters out of the spotlight. Too often a biter becomes the center of attention ("Watch out, he bites!"). If your child is in day care, be sure the provider is able to help your child communicate without biting. When your child bites to wrestle a toy from another child, show her how to share. Distract her with an equally acceptable toy or simply remove her temporarily from the play group.

Model nonaggressive behavior. Even a one year old can understand that biting hurts. You can demonstrate this by pressing your child's forearm against his upper teeth and showing him the resulting marks on his arm. Apply this self-biting demonstration immediately after your toddler bites, so that he makes the connection. But avoid doing it in a punitive or angry way. Your goal is simply to get your point across: "See, biting hurts!"

When a child bites, it is inappropriate to bite him back. Counteracting one immature behavior with another only aggravates the problem. ■

When your child's verbal skills improve and his emotions can be expressed better by language, his biting should subside (by three years of age). Biting in the child more than three years old who has good verbal skills is certainly of greater concern. In such cases professional guidance should be obtained.

The persistent aggressive behavior of an older sibling toward a young child must be stopped at all costs because of the principle of role modeling. Just as children look up to parents for affirmation of what is acceptable behavior, younger children look up to older children as their models. You don't want your one year old to learn that hitting and biting are behaviors to be modeled.

Part 2

Three to Six Years

CHAPTER 4

DISCIPLINE AND SPIRITUAL TRAINING OF THE THREE TO SIX YEAR OLD

By three years of age the child becomes aware of his total self—what he feels, what he is comfortable doing, and what he cannot yet do. He has mastered the art of using his parents as support resources and has defined his place in the family structure. By age three, the child has acquired language, motor, adaptive, and social skills. The combinations of these skills, his own basic temperament and intelligence potential, and parental guidance all come together at this stage to make up a definite person. The child who has learned these skills to his fullest potential during his first three years enters the three- to six-year-old stage ready to refine these skills. The child who has not achieved her potential in these skills during her first three years must continue to expend energy learning them; she is always trying to catch up. I do not believe that a child's basic personality (the sum total of her skills and feelings reflected in her behavior) is completely determined by this age, but it is certainly well on its way. The ability to change a behavior trait becomes increasingly difficult with advancing age.

The ages of three to six are generally smoother for both parents and child because the refinement of acquired skills usually produces less anxiety than the struggles to acquire these skills during the first three years. When you get your act together, you feel good about yourself, and I think this is true for three year olds too. The tantrums and other behavioral anxieties of the two year old were simply a manifestation of his struggle to get himself together.

By three years of age a child normally has developed enough language to communicate his desires and feelings effectively. He understands you and feels that you understand him. Since he is able to express his negative feelings with words rather than actions, his behavior generally becomes less impulsive and more directed. His abilities have finally caught up with his desires. Most three year olds have learned the important lesson of cause-and-effect relationships (child touches hot stove, child gets burned). This important milestone makes his exploring behavior less impulsive and more calculated and reasoning. Mastering language adds the finishing touch.

The attachment feeling that your child has for you enters a beautiful stage of social rapport. Your child is simply fun to talk with, to take walks with, and to play word games with. At this stage, your child may regard you as a close friend, a pal who is fun to be around. This relationship is normal and healthy as long as your roles of authority figure and spiritual trainer prevail. It is much easier to get the concept of discipline across to your child if he or she enjoys being with you.

Your child becomes aware of how much physical

abuse his developing muscles and bones can handle comfortably. As he learns to protect himself from injury, the incessant no-nos of the previous stage gradually lessen. He may retain his desire for a pleasant bedtime ritual but will probably begin to treat you to an uninterrupted night's sleep; he also has better bladder control.

Spiritual Training of the Three to Six Year Old

The ages of three to six are critical for the spiritual training of your child because this is when he or she is most receptive to learning about God. In normal childhood development most children go through several stages of learning moral values. From three to six years of age, a child accepts the values of his primary role models, his parents. Your values are his values. At no other time in a child's life will his mind be so unquestionably receptive to your values. He is still operating on the simple principle that what is important to you is important to him. Sometime after six years of age, the child matures from being completely receptive to being selective of his parents' values.

This is a normal process of spiritual maturity in which your child inwardly transfers your values to his values. (This value-transfer concept will be discussed in more detail in Chapter 7.) For this reason, this age is a prime time for spiritual training. The more values he accepts from his primary spiritual models during this stage, the greater the level of spiritual values will be from which he can select at a subsequent stage.

Parents, dwell upon this concept for a few moments. Appreciate the high level of responsibility you have at this stage to train up your child in the way he or she should go. Perhaps at no other stage of a child's development is the investment/return ratio so high.

A popular alternative to this viewpoint is that parents should remain spiritually neutral early in a child's development so that the child's mind remains open to decide for himself. Not only is this rather simplistic viewpoint contrary to Scripture (Deut. 6:6–9; Prov. 22:6), but experience has shown that it simply doesn't work. A child who is a product of spiritually neutral parents will most often, at best, turn out spiritually neutral himself. If you wait until your child is older to teach him about God, you are missing a period in his life when the ground is most fertile to sprout seeds. When he is older, you are planting the seed among thorns, and what little plants do happen to spring up may be choked out by the competition. The best time to get "in business" is at a period in your child's life when the competition is at the least.

Attachment parenting pays off. The importance of laying the foundation for spiritual training during the first three years was affirmed by a mother who had a very high-need child. She persevered through all the steps of attachment parenting previously discussed in an earlier book in this series. One day we were having one of those "it is worth it" discussions, when she said, "I feel I am just beginning to cash in." This mother meant that the attachment style of parenting in those early formative years had built up a trust relationship between parent and child and the initial two goals of early parenting had been fulfilled: knowing your child, and making your child feel right.

The early investment of attachment parenting creates an attitude of giving within the parent and an attitude of receiving within the child. These attitudes form the foundation of the trust-and-authority relationship that makes your child more receptive to all forms of training, and thus, the third goal of parenting is reached: leading your child to Christ.

Be spiritual models for your child. I like to think of spiritual training as *spiritual giving.* Spiritual giving implies that leading your child to Christ flows naturally from your own walking with Christ rather than from someone else's list of how-tos. Just as the first goals of discipline will flow naturally from attachment parenting, your spiritual discipline of your child will flow naturally from your attachment with God.

This principle of spiritual modeling is beautifully illustrated in John 15:1–2, 4.

> *I am the true vine, and My Father is the vinedresser. Every branch in Me that does not bear fruit He takes away; and every branch that bears fruit He prunes, that it may bear more fruit. . . . Abide in Me, and I in you. As the branch cannot bear fruit of itself, unless it abides in the vine, neither can you, unless you abide in Me.*

As spiritual leader of our family, I have adopted this passage as God's clear mandate for the relationship between us and our Father. We can extend this passage to signify the relationship between the spiritual leader of the family (usually, but not always, the father) and the children. If the parents remain in Christ and Christ remains in the parents, the parents become an extension of Christ to their children. When the children are older spiritually, they can develop direct relationships with Christ and abide in Him.

When your children accept the message of John 15:1–4 and accept Christ into their lives, you have achieved the goal of spiritual training. A child's accepting Christ directly as he gets older is much easier if he has first accepted Christ indirectly through his parents at an earlier age. Just as a mother who is one with her child is naturally giving her child her own milk, parents who are truly at one with Christ will naturally give spiritual milk to their children (Heb. 5:12–13).

What about newborn Christians who have not laid this spiritual foundation during their first two years of parenthood? Is it too late? No! Just as early bonding with a newborn gives you a head start in parenting, an early spiritual foundation gives you a head start in spiritual training. The later you begin, the greater your commitment must be in order to catch up. As you are catching up in your spiritual growth, you probably will have to go through a long how-to stage before your spiritual training naturally flows from you into your child.

Teaching Your Child About God

Your child's first three years of spiritual training basically teach him that God is an important Person. In the three- to six-year-old stage, this concept is carried one step further: God is an important Person because . . . At this point many Christian parents need help: What do I teach my child about God? How do I teach him? How much can my child understand about God at this stage?

Most of your teaching at this stage (and at every

other stage) is in your example for your child. Remember, the three to six year old is still operating from the basis that what is important to you is important to him. You can tell him a thousand times how important the Bible is, but if he seldom sees you reading from your Bible and praying, very little of your teaching actually will sink in.

Next, use one of the most powerful principles of learning: repetition. God used this principle in Deuteronomy 6 when He told people to saturate their child's environment with His Word. Not just a five-minute bedtime prayer or a one-hour Sunday school lesson. By example and repetition begin to teach your young child about God.

Very early in your child's spiritual training, set some goals. What do you want your child to learn about God especially at the three- to six-year-old stage? To answer this question, let's consult the Manufacturer's Handbook. God told us how and what to teach our children. The following Scriptures offer some basics to teach your child at this stage.

1. *"Love the LORD your God with all your heart, with all your soul, and with all your strength"* (Deut. 6:5). In the New Testament Jesus reinforced the importance of this verse by repeating this concept. I emphasize this verse because Jesus emphasized it. When the teachers of the Law asked Jesus which is the most important commandment, He stated, "Love the LORD" (Mark 12:30). So, the first concept to teach your child is to love the Lord.

But how do you teach love to your child? To answer this question, open the Book again to Deuteronomy where God said that the next step is to make this love of God part of yourself: "And these words [to love

95

the Lord] which I command you today shall be in your heart" (6:6). The next step is to "teach them [to love the Lord] to your children" (11:19). Get the concept of loving God into your child by any means. The more your child knows about Him, the more he will learn to love Him.

Our four year old, Hayden, told me she loves me more than she loves God because she knows me more than she knows God. It is certainly easier for a child to love his parents more than God because he can see and feel and hear his parents. But God is still an abstraction to a young child. Love related to how a child feels about his parents is usually a simple feeling such as, "I want to be near that person who does good things for me, who takes care of me, who makes me feel good, who is so big and strong and powerful that he can chop down trees and fix bicycles. I miss him when I am not near him." It is vitally important that a child love his parents whom he can see so that he can learn to love his God whom he can't see. A child's parents can help him know and love God by pointing out that God made everything and everyone because He loves us.

By using a picture Bible, a three- to six-year-old child can learn about Jesus more easily than he can learn about God. These two can gradually become one as your child matures. A young child can learn that Jesus loves little children (the song "Jesus Loves the Little Children" is a favorite at this age), that He protects little children, and that He is kind and gentle. Jesus is God's Son, which makes him God too. Young children picture God as Michelangelo did—an all-powerful grandfather who made "Mommy and Daddy and me."

2. *Fear the Lord and walk in His ways.* In Deuteronomy 10:12 God said, "What does the LORD your God require of you, but to fear the LORD your God, to walk in all His ways." Your first goal as Christian parents is to teach your young children the concept of fearing God. Several times in Scripture the concepts of love and fear coexist. Usually by four years of age a child can understand that God is a powerful Person who makes rules (just as his or her parents make rules). The biblical term *fear* really refers to an awed respect for the power and wisdom of God. This concept of fear rounds out the concept of love. In reality how a child learns about God is paralleled with how he learns about his parents—to love and fear his parents (to have a healthy respect for his parents). Again, through the use of a picture Bible, the child less than six years old can learn respect for the power of God as she grasps the biblical concept of sin. At this age the child can learn that the Person who loves also disciplines. If presented properly to a young child, the story of Adam and Eve, or of Moses and the Red Sea, and the New Testament miracles can convey to him the power of God—power to love, to heal, and to discipline.

Learning the concept of sin is a major turning point in the young child's discipline. The child less than six years old can grasp this simple notion of sin: "This big Person whom Mom and Dad call 'God' makes rules. I can't see Him, but He sees me. He knows when I do bad things even if Mom and Dad don't, but He still loves me anyway just like Mom and Dad do." You may introduce the teachings of the Ten Commandments to the child between four and six years old but keep them in simple, everyday terms: worship God in a special way on Sunday, obey your parents, be kind to your friends and don't hurt them, tell the truth, don't take other children's toys. By introducing to your child the concepts of fear, sin, and God's rules, you are laying the foundation of conscience building that matures in the next stage of development when he or she is between six and twelve years of age. The child less than six should be able to feel the beginning of a conscience: "I feel good when I do the right thing; I don't feel good when I do the wrong thing." Both your laws and God's laws should be consistently repeated and presented to the young child when he is most receptive to the concepts of right and wrong.

3. *"Love your neighbor as yourself"* (Mark 12:31). Jesus said this is the second greatest commandment after loving the Lord. One of the major milestones a three to six year old has is the development of peer relationships. Three year olds show a desire to refine their social attitudes and show varying degrees of social readiness. The three year old evolves from parallel play patterns to a more cooperative play pattern of sharing other children's toys. The three year old becomes more comfortable in peer play groups of varying sizes, and it is in these play groups that some young children show behaviors of pushing and shoving until they have established themselves in the pecking order and learned what is socially acceptable behavior within the peer group. Demanding, possessive, assertive, and withdrawn behaviors are all realistic expectations at this age. The "law of the jungle" or "may the most assertive child win" is usually the most typical behavior needing modification in these peer groups.

Squabbles over toys are to be expected at this age because possession means ownership to a young child. If sharing is a major play problem for your child, ask children to bring a few toys of their own when they come to visit. Capitalize on your child's natural desire to play with another child's toys. As she grabs someone else's toy, another child will grab her toy. Have a rule that even though it is "her" toy when she is alone, in a play group, if a toy is put down, another child is allowed to pick it up and play with it. She will learn to give a toy to get a toy, and eventually, sharing can be the law of the jungle.

How much more meaningful it is to a child if the "love your neighbor" rule is introduced instead of the "may the most assertive child win" rule. At this stage, again with the use of picture books, show a child a picture of Jesus, saying he should love and be kind to the children he plays with. In the middle of toy squabbles it often helps to take a few minutes out and encourage children to put their arms around each other, saying, "Love each other. Jesus wants us to love each other." Young children need to learn that this is not a give-me-give-me world but that sharing and giving are the Christian way.

A common discipline problem facing you at this stage occurs when your child is acted upon aggressively and wronged. Should she be encouraged to fight back? In my opinion, it is healthy to teach children to be assertive but not aggressive. A child is assertive when he protects his own territory; a child is aggressive when she infringes upon others' territory. A parent often states, "I don't want him to grow up to be a pansy." Being assertive does seem to be within the realm of Christian discipline, and perhaps assertiveness toward the aggressor by the child who is transgressed upon is a valuable social lesson. Since Christ did stress meekness and the attitude of turning the other cheek, parents should teach their children that physical assertiveness should be followed by an act of love. In Galatians 5:14–15 Paul gave some guidance about handling aggressive behavior and squabbles: "'You shall love your neighbor as yourself.' But if you bite and devour one another, beware lest you be consumed by one another!"

4. Pray that the Holy Spirit will fill your child (Gal. 5:22–25). The desired result in Christian discipline is to impress God's Word upon your child to such a degree that his or her entire behavior is directed by the inner power God has promised—the Holy Spirit. What a magnificent level of behavior on which to be! In Galatians 5:17–18 Paul reminded people of the bent toward evil that is present to varying degrees in everyone: "For the flesh lusts against the Spirit, and the Spirit against the flesh; and these are contrary to one another, so that you do not do the things that you wish. But if you are led by the Spirit, you are not under the law." After mentioning many common human sins, Paul went on to warn, "Those who practice such things will not inherit the kingdom of God" (v. 21). The ultimate goal of Christian discipline is for your child to inherit the kingdom of God, and a Spirit-filled Christian life is the best path to this kingdom.

Parents, pray daily for the Spirit to come into your child. It is humbling for Christian parents to realize that the fruit of the Holy Spirit in Galatians 5:22–23—love, joy, peace, longsuffering, kindness, goodness, faithfulness, gentleness, and self-control—will not develop in their children by their efforts alone. The earlier in a child's life you can pray these qualities into your child, the more effective your child's Christian discipline will be.

Teach your child to pray and to praise. Between

three and six years of age a child learns to talk with God. This is the stage at which a child should know how to pray and why to pray. A child's attitude toward prayer at this stage can determine the attitude about prayer parents are all hoping their children will have—the desire to pray. The following specific guidelines will help you teach your young child to pray.

1. *Use short, simple phrases* containing ideas and terms that you want your child to pick up: "Father . . . I thank You . . . I love You . . . I'm sorry . . . be with me . . . I ask for . . . I praise You." Most prayers of young children contain "give mes," but that is the nature of young children and certainly God understands this tendency. However, parents should teach their children to add the concept of praise and love and thanksgiving to their prayers in addition to what they ask for.

2. *Teach your child to pray for others.* This custom makes their prayers less selfish and sets the stage for Christian fellowship at an older age.

3. *Pray often.* Before going to bed and after getting up in the morning are the two most important times to pray with your child. You want your child to begin each day with God and end each day with God; and in between times he or she should pray as often as the need or desire arises.

4. *Pray spontaneously.* Be vigilant for "openers": a child is hurt during play, a tantrum is out of control, or a child's behavior has deteriorated. Take advantage of these spontaneous occurrences, and take a few minutes to follow up by saying, "Now let's pray about this," or "Let's talk with God about this." This spontaneous prayer teaches your child that at any time during day and night he can and should talk to his heavenly Father.

5. *Encourage Scripture memorization.* Give your child short, one-sentence memory verses and include the Scripture reference: "God is love" (1 John 4:8). Young children love the challenge of a memory verse, and their young minds are receptive to this exercise. Discuss the meaning of these verses with your child, then encourage him to relate the meaning back to you. Memory without meaning has limited teaching value to a child.

6. *Acknowledge answered prayer.* Be sure to follow up on answered prayer requests with your young child. He or she needs to learn prayer power at this age. The follow-up of apparently "unanswered" prayer is more important for the older child, who can be taught better to pray according to God's will.

7. *Let your child hear praises.* It is important for you to model praise and prayer for your child. If he hears sincere "thank You, Lords" and "praise Gods," he gets the idea that you are constantly walking with God, and he will want to walk with Him too.

8. *Model prayer and family devotions.* Children learn to pray as they hear their parents pray. Prayer demonstrates to the young child a sense of the reality of God; prayer gives her a sense of security that she is talking to Someone very important who hears her. Parents often learn from their children's prayers about the people and things that are most important to them. This is one way parents can learn about the special problems and needs their children have. Older children's prayer requests are particularly telling since older children are more private about their needs.

Children enjoy using memorized prayers since the rhythm of these prayers appeals to them. Use memorized prayers as little as possible, since this kind of prayer from adults tends to be rattled off without sincerity. Children are very quick to pick up the vibrations that you are insincere and not at ease with prayer. Although the young child should be encouraged to pray among family members, some children do not welcome being put on the spot for a prayer performance, especially among strangers. It is more important that a child learn to focus his attention on God during prayer than on the group in which he or she is praying.

9. *Teach Scripture.* A primary goal in your teaching Scripture at this stage is for your child to achieve a positive attitude toward the Bible. This is more important than how many verses he memorizes or how many stories he learns. Again, role modeling is your most effective Bible teacher. As your child sees God the way you do, he also sees the Bible as you do: "That big Book must be very important. Mom and Dad are always reading from it, praying from it, and talking about it. That Book tells us about important people who say and do important things. I want to learn about those people too." More than at any other age the three to six year old is observant of his or her parents' values.

In the beginning when you teach your young child about the Bible, wait for openers. If your child sees you reading the Bible often enough he will eventually, and of his own free will, climb up onto your lap and ask you to read to him too. This is especially true if you are reading the Bible as a family; he doesn't want to be left out. Capitalize on the interest he has initiated by inviting him with a very childlike reception such as, "Daddy was reading a neat story. Would you like to hear it?" After you have told him the story (pick one that is at his level, such as the baby Jesus story), say, "Would you like your own book about Jesus?" There are many picture Bibles written for all levels of child development. You may find that much of your Scripture-reading time is spent reading to your child out of his picture Bible. This is not wasted Scripture time for you, since you may be surprised at how much more you may learn about the Bible by getting down to your child's level, seeing God through his eyes, and giving simple answers to his questions. Jesus said, "Unless you are converted and become as little children, you will by no means enter the kingdom of heaven" (Matt. 18:3).

Play-acting is also a good way to teach Scripture to children at this age; they can dress up like various Bible characters and put on a family skit. Christmas and Easter are particularly valuable times for play-acting from Scripture. Children can dress up and participate in the event of Christ's birth. And, of course, you have all the little props, such as a doll for baby Jesus, a little wagon or crib for a manger, and an assortment of household animals.

Prescheduled time and structure for teaching prayer and Scripture to a young child are not as effective as spontaneous prayer and Bible reading when the opportunity arises. Young children live from moment to moment, neither thinking about the past nor anticipating the future. Prayer and Scripture teaching are much more meaningful when they are based upon a sudden event that occurs while you are simply having fun together. For example, a walk through a garden or the woods with your child will open up a variety of opportunities to relate God to nature. You may see a beautiful sunset and stop and say, "Bobby, let's thank God for the pretty red sky." After you have prayed, your child is likely to ask a simple question, "Did God make the sun?" which allows you the opportunity to talk about God and creation. When your child gives you a simple opener, reply with a simple answer. Don't exhaust him with long and complicated answers because he is likely to tune out and become less motivated to get into that subject again.

When teaching your child a certain scriptural passage, identify the central point. A child cannot take in multiple important points all at once and is liable to become confused. Remember, creating a positive attitude toward Scripture is your prime motive at this age, not the content of information. By consistently hearing a second language in the home, a child naturally picks it up. With consistent Bible teaching and by talking about God the way God told us to do in Deuteronomy 6:7–9, the young child takes on God's language as his "second language."

Christian parents who are sincerely trying to teach their children about God often wonder how much is sinking in and to what level. More often than not, if the message is taught sincerely and lived in role modeling, more penetrates your child than you probably think. For example, I heard my four-year-old daughter say, "I have Jesus in my heart." I asked her what that meant, and she responded, "I love Him." I said, "Is Jesus really in your heart?" and she surprised me by the answer, "No, but His Spirit is." I felt comfortable that she had in her "heart" what ought to be there based on her own level of spiritual development and understanding.

Parents, beware of the "floater"—the child who floats through your biblical teaching pretending to understand everything but actually perceiving very little. Children pick up vocabulary very easily. They learn to talk a good game. I've heard the story of preschool children who heard a sermon about inviting Jesus into their hearts; one child said, "I have Jesus in my heart," and the other child said, "I have Jesus in my tummy." Probably the child who thought Jesus was in his tummy really had more of a concept of Jesus' being *inside* of him than the other child did.

For this reason it will help you to have a checklist to see where your child is in his or her spiritual growth by the age of six. This checklist is measured in relation to where you want your child to be. Periodically check where your child is in relation to the following goals.

1. To love and fear God
2. To love our neighbors as ourselves
3. To obey God and our parents
4. To practice self-control

Teaching Your Child About Jesus

A child less than six tends to confuse the terms *Jesus* and *God* and is just as likely to say "Jesus made me" as "God made me." If you show him a "picture" of Jesus, he is likely to answer that the person is Jesus. Since there are no actual pictures it is not known what Jesus looked like. But I see no problem with this. Our children have many picture books and Jesus looks a bit different in each one. Our children have never been confused by this or even have mentioned it. They can always pick out which one is Jesus because He is the One the child is drawn to from the story in the text. If a child sees a picture of a grandfatherly looking figure he is likely to answer that the individual is God. When teaching your child about Jesus, you should emphasize

His humanity because children can relate to this. By your reading stories about Jesus, the child can learn that Jesus is kind, patient, and gentle and that He especially loves little children. Young children are more likely to view God as a disciplinarian, a father-authority figure who passes judgment on them.

A child less than six can grasp the concept that Jesus is the Son of God. He understands the concept of a son and that Jesus was a man, but do not confuse him with the concept of the Trinity at this age. It is more important for the child to be comfortable first with the humanity of Christ. Introduce the concept of the deity of Christ later. Basically you want the young child to be concerned with what Jesus teaches, what He does for us, and what He tells us to do. Then later on when the child matures, he can be more concerned with who Jesus is. A six year old can grasp the fact that if Jesus is the Son of God, He must be God too.

By first teaching the humanity of Jesus, you are teaching your child as He taught His disciples. First they learned that He was a powerful and righteous man. Only later did they come to see Him as the Son of God. Christ seemed to realize the difficulty that even adults would have grasping His deity, since He stated that revelation from His Father was necessary to grasp this concept: "Blessed are you, Simon Bar-Jonah, for flesh and blood has not revealed this to you, but My Father who is in heaven" (Matt. 16:17). At this point in the spiritual training of your child, pray that God will reveal directly to your child's receptive mind a clear understanding of what He wants your child to understand at this age.

When teaching your child about Jesus, relate His life to the real life of the child: Jesus was born as a baby.

He grew up in a house, and He helped His earthly father work as a carpenter. When Jesus was older, a teenager (relate this age to a teenager your child knows, an older sibling or family friend), He taught people about His Father, God in heaven. When Jesus was a grown man, He told us the right things to do and the wrong things to do. Here mention the commandments in simple terms that the child can understand and emphasize the two great commandments of the New Testament: love God and love your neighbor. Teach your child that many people accepted what Jesus taught, followed Him, obeyed His commandments, and loved Him. Those people were called "Christians" because they were like Christ. Teach that Mommy and Daddy are Christians, and as he gets to know Jesus better and accepts Him into his life, he will be a Christian too. At that point you may be fortunate to get a response of, "I want to be a Christian too." This beautiful opener gives you the opportunity to tell your child what it means to be a Christian after he has given his life to Jesus and invited Him into his heart. Tell him it means he (1) loves God; (2) learns about God by reading His Book; (3) loves his neighbor as himself (explain in child's terms); and (4) obeys God and his parents.

Once the child has reached this level of reasoning, he is ready to understand that being a Christian has both responsibilities and rewards. Jesus promised us that He would take us to heaven when we accept Him as our Savior. Read together John 3:16; 14:1–6; and 1 John 5:11–12. A young child is reward oriented: "I will go to heaven because this is what Jesus promises, and He always tells the truth." His concept of heaven is most likely to be materialistic, simply because it is a place where everything is free and everyone feels good all the time. Come to think about it, some adult concepts of heaven are not much more mature than a child's.

The concept of salvation can be taught to a child sometime around the age of five or six. At this stage a child is going to wonder why Jesus was born and why He came here. This is the time to teach your child about the concept of sin. Explain to him (with the help of a picture Bible) that Adam and Eve sinned by disobeying God. At this point you are driving home the concept of disobedience. Adam and Eve, God's first children, did something wrong (they sinned), and as a result they suffered by losing the good things God had given them. Next you can introduce the concept that Jesus died on the cross to ask His Father to forgive us for all the sins we have ever done and will ever do.

The young child will have a limited understanding of repentance, but he does know that once he has "repented" (gone to his room for a while after doing something wrong), Mommy totally wipes the slate clean. This simple thought prepares the way for introducing the concept of how Jesus wiped the slate clean for everyone.

Remember that your child is "now" oriented. Teach mostly for the present, what Jesus means to him now and what he needs now at his stage of development. The best way to prepare a child for the future concepts of God is to meet his needs now.

The old axiom, "You learn by teaching," is especially true when you teach your children about God. A fringe benefit of teaching them is that your own beliefs are tested and your faith is strengthened. As you teach little children, you begin to see God through their eyes, just as they see God through your eyes.

Perhaps in commanding you to teach your children, God also speaks to you through them.

This concept, that parents learn as they teach their children, is especially true for the parent who is a new Christian or who is sincerely trying to strengthen a weakened faith. The ideal is for parents to be rooted firmly in their Christian faith in order to impress Christian teachings upon their children. However, it is unwise to think, *I'll wait until I become the perfect Christian parent model, and then I'll teach my child about Christ.* For many Christian parents, spiritual growth is a slow and steady maturing process. A child cannot afford to wait for his parents to get their act together. The principle of Christian childhood education is very similar to the principle of childhood education in general as described by Dr. Maria Montessori. Dr. Montessori said that preschool children have what she called "sensitive periods" in which their little minds are most receptive to various types of learning. In my opinion, ages three to six are the years in which a child is most sensitive and receptive to Christian teaching. Parents, please don't miss this chance.

Some parents may sincerely feel that they are lukewarm Christians as adults because they had no in-depth Christian teaching during their own sensitive periods as children. Therefore, they are determined not to make this mistake with their own children.

Even though you are struggling to strengthen your Christianity with prayer and consultation, give your child your very best. As long as you are sincerely trying and praying for God's help, you will succeed. Be sincere. Avoid portraying Jesus as a mythical figure who will help keep your child on the straight and narrow path. Children outwardly seem to accept Santa Claus but inwardly and intuitively feel he is not real. If God is presented insincerely, He is likely to fade into obscurity just like Santa Claus and the Easter bunny. Give your child as much of the "real thing" as you can.

Establishing and Improving Family Devotions

Through your modeling, you child will perceive that the Christian way of life is so attractive and feels so right that he or she cannot help realizing it is the right way to go. Family devotions are an important part of the spiritual training and devotional life of your child. However, for most families it is difficult to set aside an exclusive time of the day for the Lord. There is stiff competition for your time and also for the minds of your children. Family life is usually a series of "I gotta gos" or what Dr. James Dobson calls "routine panic." In our own busy home, we struggle with the concept of daily family devotions. This section will give you some practical suggestions on how to improve your family devotions.

The Lord must have priority in spite of all the protests: "But, Dad, the game is about to start on TV . . ."; "I'm late for . . ."; "Do we have to?" The first concept you need to convey to your family is the importance of family devotions. It's important to set aside some time each day for family worship. Throughout a child's life, he will be called upon to set priorities and to follow his conscience and God's commandments rather than his own impulses. The younger the child is, the better it is for him to learn that time with God has priority over any earthly commitment or desire. If you have introduced your child to family devotions and spent time in prayer and Scripture early on in child-hood, these devotions will be received better when your child is older.

If you are just starting family devotions, the father must assume the role of spiritual leader and stress the importance of family devotions to his children: "God has blessed our family and we must come together to thank Him; according to Matthew 18:20, God is with us whenever two or more are gathered in His name. We are going to take ten minutes after the evening meal each night to pray together as a family." With such an introduction you have told your children why family devotions are important, and you have modeled the concept that family devotions are important to you. Then you must rely on the Holy Spirit to make this time come alive. Spirit-filled prayer can be irresistible, so learn how to let the Spirit lead these devotions through you.

We have found that the best time for our family devotions is after the evening meal. Everyone is already gathered at the table, thus reducing the start-up time. A pleasant evening meal should set the stage and atti-tude for the devotions to follow. This meal is often the only time in the day when all family members are together. It should be a happy time; a time when all family members are in tune with one another's happen-ings of the day. Mealtimes are for communication, not for correction.

On weekends and holidays consider having family devotions after breakfast. Starting the day with God sets the tone for the entire day. If interest in family devo-tions seems to wane, occasionally hold your family de-votions as a part of a special outing such as to a local park. On family trips, devotions can be held during the car ride. The important thing is that your family does pray together, not where you pray together.

Parents, do not feel you have to convince your children that devotions are "fun." Children are already preoccupied with the idea that everything has to be fun. Devotions are sacred; early in their lives children should learn to delay their need for instant gratification. Family devotions are not in the same category as a family TV program.

Keep your devotions brief, approximately ten minutes to begin with, and increase their length according to the attention span and interest level of your children. As your devotions become more meaningful to your children, or in a time of particularly high need and when they are more attentive, the length of the family devotions can be increased. Consistency is more important than duration. It is more important to have them every night than to wait until there is enough time to have a "long" devotion. Avoid "squeeze" devotions. This special time with God should not be made to fit in between other commitments; other commitments should be made to fit around your family devotions. This level of priority is an important concept for your children to perceive.

How can you hold your child's interest? Many children, especially those younger than five years old, have short attention spans and like to fidget. To minimize this, insist on removing all toys and distractions from the devotion table. Giving everyone a "part" will hold the attention span of children. Even if your child who is younger than four years old appears to get nothing out of the devotions, persevere. If your child gets only one message—that family devotions are important because God is important to your family—then your efforts are worthwhile. Even if a young child does not actually understand all the words, he will perceive the attitudes of the prayers and phrases. Try to put the children's part early in the family devotions, which gets them involved right away. Ask your children to contribute suggestions on how to run family devotions, and you may be amazed at what they come up with. Our seven year old, Peter, suggested that we take the phone off the hook during our devotional time, and we all concurred that it was a terrific idea.

Every family member could have a Bible, a notepad, and a pencil. The Living Bible, a children's edition, or a picture Bible is good for young children. You could maintain a prayer calendar to write down specific prayer requests, and later on, write down when and how they were answered—praise God for answered prayers. Family devotion could contain the following elements.

1. *Opening prayer.* The father, as the spiritual leader of the home, should open the devotions with a prayer. This prayer should remind the family of Jesus' promise, "Where two or three are gathered together in My name, I am there in the midst of them" (Matt. 18:30). An opening prayer could be, "Father, thank You that You are with our family during this special time. We thank You that You hear our prayers; open our hearts to Your message." Children often listen to cue words during prayer. This simple prayer conveys to them the presence of Christ within the prayer group, and it also conveys to your children that attitude of peace and tranquillity they need in order to listen to the Lord.

2. *Scripture lesson.* Scripture can be incorporated into family worship in many ways. One way is to cover certain books of the Bible by reading sequential passages each night. However, we have found that the specific-topics approach works best for our family because it relates scriptural lessons to specific family needs. Specific topics tend to hold the interest of children better than sequential scriptural passages. If you choose this topical approach, you can list scriptural lessons that relate to the general needs as well as the specific needs of your family. Examples of these are love, patience, kindness, faith, prayer, obedience, charity, and sin. The family member who is assigned the Scripture reading for that devotion is given the Bible concordance and asked to choose several verses on the specific topic. The topic of love, for example, would give you enough scriptural passages for several weeks of devotions. Children seven or eight years of age or older can usually be given these verses to read to the family. Young children less than eight years of age may be given memory verses, since young children usually can memorize much better than they can read. Follow the Scripture reading or memory recital with a discussion of the meaning of the verse and its relevance to your family. The Bible is not only to be read and memorized: it is also to be understood and followed (2 Tim. 3:16–17).

3. *Sharing of needs and prayer requests.* The father can ask if there are any prayer requests, and each family member can share his or her request with the group. Prayer requests serve many purposes. They convey to children that prayer is important. Christians should bring their requests and needs before other Christians, especially their own families. The ability to share a need sets the stage for a beautiful Christian family attitude. Sharing leads to caring, and caring leads to more *agape*

115

love and more *phileo* love among family members. Learning to pray for others begins this way.

Prayer requests during family devotions allow an avenue of communication because some children feel less threatened opening up their hearts to God than to their parents or other family members. In our large family, the prayer calendar helps us take inventory of each child's specific needs. Children often have rather simple requests such as winning a ball game. They should be spared the heavy burdens that usually form the basis of adult prayer requests.

Acknowledge each prayer request. A parent can pray for all requests or encourage each child to pray for another child's need. Parents, encourage your children to care and pray for one another. Sensitivity to each others' needs, the "I care" attitude, is one of the most important dynamics for the Christian family. Remember the principles of modeling? Parents model for the children; older children model for the younger children. The modeling of attitudes and commitments to family devotions filters down from the older to the younger. If the interest of the young children periodically wanes, and it usually does, convey to the older children the responsibility they have to encourage their younger brothers and sisters.

4. *Praise for answered prayer.* Periodically bring out the prayer calendar and thank God for answered prayer. Children need to learn the power of prayer and that prayer requests may not always be answered in ways they want them to be answered. What a wonderful way to learn that God, their Father, really does know what is best for them and meets their needs in ways they would not have expected or imagined or chosen.

5. *The closing prayer* should be offered by the father as the spiritual leader of the home. Fathers, assume authority in your prayers, for example, "Father, we have come before You as a family with love in our voices and in our hearts; we thank You for the love we have for You and for one another. Help us to care for one another and pray for one another's needs that we have shared in this special time together as a family. We bring our requests to You, Father, in full belief that You are present in this house to hear us and to help us."

Spiritual Training Improves Your Child's Self-Esteem

A child's attitudes and behavior mirror his or her self-esteem. The first stage in developing your child's self-esteem is to practice the principles of attachment parenting during his or her first two years. The child receives the message that his parents love him and that he is important to them. In the period from three to six years of age you carry these principles of parenting one step further into your spiritual parenting. The child learns: "God loves me, I am important to God." The child who has sincerely invited Christ into her heart has a head start toward the development of a good self-esteem. The need for this continuum of love from parents, love from God, and love of self is especially true of a difficult or high-need child. The difficult child who has learned to feel and accept the love of her parents has a head start in receiving the love of God. This feeling can be reinforced by parents' instructing their children that God has made them in His image (Gen. 1:27) and that Christ shows special love for children (Mark 10:13–16).

A child who knows that the Sprit dwells within her and has a personal relationship with God her Father is well on her way toward developing Spirit-directed Christian living. This feeling that "God loves me" in the younger child gradually matures into the older child's feeling, "I'm right with God; I feel right; I act right." This feeling is the ultimate goal of Christian discipline—that righteousness means being right with God, based on salvation through Jesus Christ. Hebrews 5:13–14 states: "For everyone who partakes only of milk is unskilled in the word of righteousness, for he is a babe. But solid food belongs to those who are of full age, that is, those who by reason of use have their senses exercised to discern both good and evil." Matthew 6:33 states: "But seek first the kingdom of God and His righteousness, and all these things shall be added to you."

■ Helping Your Child Build a Healthy Self-Image

Throughout life, your child will be exposed to people and events that contribute to her self-worth (builders) and to others that chip away at it (breakers). The key to growing a child with a healthy self-image is to expose your child to many more builders than breakers and, of course, become a builder yourself. Here's how.

Mirror positive messages. Much of a child's self-esteem comes not only from what the child perceives about herself, but how she thinks others perceive her. Parents are constantly giving children messages, or value judgments, such as "good girl" or "bad boy." Simply put, a child's self-image is a reflection and a collection of the messages the child receives. Periodically take inventory of what messages your child receives from yourself and other persons of significance in her life. Do you and others reflect predominately positive messages, or predominately negative ones? Do you expose your child to lots of "builders" and help him work through the "breakers"?

Children's behavior is shaped, for better or for worse, by the messages they receive from those around them. From these, children perceive how others view them and form assumptions about themselves. It's a fact of human nature that people react to "good" children with more positive messages. Children who are not so easy to be around are more likely to receive negative messages about themselves. If children sense that those around them don't like them, they eventually learn not to like themselves, and they enter the cycle of poor self-esteem. They perceive that people think they are bad, they believe they are bad, so they continue to act badly. Some challenging children do not bring out the best in adults, and you have to make a conscious effort to be positive. We value and praise "good babies" and "easy children." The convenient child is likely to get more positive strokes from parents and teachers than the one who extracts every ounce of parental energy and requires creative teaching. Fill your child's developing mind with messages about what's "right" with him rather than what's "wrong."

Discover your child's special something. Over the years of parenting eight children and in counseling thousands of other families in pediatric practice, we've noticed a phenomenon we call "the carryover principle." Success breeds success. If a child succeeds in one endeavor, this carries over into her overall self-worth, such as the star athlete also gets a boost in academic performance. Recognize your child's special talents, and help her build on them, and then watch the whole person blossom.

Beware of value-by-comparison. In our measuring-and-testing society, children's skills—and therefore their value—are measured relative to others. Your child may bat an exceptional .400 on the softball team, but she will feel inadequate if her teammates are batting .500. Be sure your child believes you value her because of who she is, not for how she performs.

Surround you child with builders. Screen your child's persons of significance in her life: relatives, coaches, teachers, religious leaders, scout leaders, and friends. It's up to parents to screen out those who pull down their child's character and encourage those who build it.

Monitor school influences on your child. Some schools can be hazardous to a child's self-esteem. If your child is doing poorly at school, guard against your child being tagged with unfair labels, such as "dumb," "learning disabled," or "slow." Oftentimes, these untrue and unfair labels are predominately a mismatch between the style of teaching and your child's individual style of learning.

Parents, don't feel that self-esteem is one more thing you are required to give your child, sort of like regular meals and a winter jacket. You don't need a degree in psychology to raise a confident child. Reflect that you truly value your child; then sit back and enjoy the person whose self-esteem is developing naturally. ■

Teaching Impulse Control and Delayed Gratification

As Christian parents, you must help your children control their impulses and delay their gratification. It is not enough to instruct them in the teachings of Christ; you must make practical, day-by-day applications. You need to teach them that they can't have everything they want. Today's children are growing up in a world where they are constantly being told of material things they need to "fulfill them." For a child to be fulfilled with the things of Christ, he must learn at a very young age to be able to say no to the things of the world, but this is difficult for a young child (and for many adults). The inability to control their impulses and to say no to their sensual desires is one of the main weaknesses that get many adults into trouble. Self-control is one of the fruits of the Holy Spirit (Gal. 5:23).

By nature the young child is impulsive. He is also programmed to have his needs met consistently and predictably because they have been met in that way all during infancy. Fulfillment of needs is necessary for the feeling of rightness in the tiny baby and older infant.

As the infant matures into the child from three to six years of age, you will be more able to differentiate between his needs and his wants. Throughout Scripture, fasting is mentioned along with prayer as necessary to becoming a mature Christian. Fasting for a long time is medically unwise for young children who are prone to low blood sugar and behavioral changes. However, fasting to a young child can simply mean saying no to a certain craving. Teaching the child the spiritual basis for saying no adds a more meaningful dimension to the concept of fasting, which will not be very popular.

For example, you and your child are walking by an ice-cream parlor, and he makes the usual plea for an ice-cream cone with a double scoop. This opportunity falls into the category of "teachable moments" in which you might say, "John, I know you would like to have a double scoop ice-cream cone and I would like one too; but I have a neat idea. Let's talk about it. Sometimes Jesus asks us to give up something very special that we want because when we say no to having it we are stronger inside. Jesus calls this 'fasting.' I'm not going to have an ice-cream cone even though I really would like to have one. So why don't you have only one scoop, and we both will show Jesus how strong we are." Impulse controls start gradually. Rather than asking John to give up the entire ice-cream cone, start with one scoop and the next time he may volunteer to give up the entire ice-cream cone. Or you may say, "Let's wait until tomorrow for that ice-cream cone." The concept of tomorrow seems like an eternity to a young child.

The more you suggest delayed gratification for simple things, the easier it is to build up to major sacrifices and the more disciplined your child will become in controlling his wants. For the young child, simply giving up the fulfillment of certain cravings, such as ice-cream cones, is beautiful in the eyes of God. This helps the child accept the concept of true fasting more easily when he becomes an adult.

Other Ways to Encourage Desirable Behavior

Disciplining your child is giving him or her a sense of direction. Spiritual training is the first and foremost step in discipline, but there are other ways in which you can design your child's environment to encourage his or her desirable behavior.

A primary behavior director is building a sense of responsibility and impulse control in the young child. When your three year old has accomplished most of the basic skills of childhood, she needs some direction about what to do with them. If her skills are not channeled in the right direction, she will deviate into trouble. This is often the last stage at which a child will voluntarily want to help Mommy and Daddy around the house. The three to six year old does not often distinguish between work and play. In fact, to a young child, doing any task with a parent is play; doing it alone is work. Start building responsibility and impulse control with "play chores": helping Mommy and Daddy do dishes, sweeping the floor, picking up clothes (presented as the game "let's tidy up"). By involving the young child in household chores, you are helping him or her develop work attitudes and habits at a young age. In later stages, most children see work as somewhat undesirable, and they often rebel. Your main goal at this stage is to shape the attitude about work, not to get the floor clean.

As you encourage your child to work with you,

gradually require him to do specific jobs on his own and hold him accountable for their completion. At this stage you are building on a principle in child discipline, the privilege/responsibility ratio: Increasing privileges means increasing responsibilities. When the privileges are unearned and multiply faster than the responsibilities, discipline is not balanced and the child is headed for trouble. Some people call this "spoiling" a child.

Wisely choose jobs for your three year old. Keep the task short, simple, and achievable. Be certain he can see immediately the fruits of his labors. A good choice is having him load a basket of laundry into the washer. The child gets his specific instructions, the task is short, he starts with a full basket, he quickly sees his accomplishment, and he is praised genuinely for the empty basket. Room tidiness should be required. Remember, from two to four years of age is a sensitive period for the concept of order. Child-level pegs for hanging up his clothes, drawers for storing, and shelf compartments for filing toys teach the child to respect an orderly environment. If you are not sensitive to the child's need for an orderly environment, she will drift off into the lazy custom of piles of toys and clothes all over the floor. The responsibility for her own belongings must be one of your nonnegotiable mandates of housekeeping. Insist on a young child's completing the job well—putting away *all* her toys with your help if necessary—and then acknowledge a job well done. Remember the principle of positive reinforcement: desirable behavior, if rewarded, will continue throughout your parenting years.

CHAPTER 5

SEXUALITY EDUCATION IN EARLY CHILDHOOD

■ "When do I start talking to my child about sex?" is a common question parents ask. I reply, "You begin giving sexual messages to your child the minute he or she is born." In this section, I will use the term *sexuality*, which implies not only the physical aspects of sex education but also the emotions and attitudes accompanying these physical changes.

Modeling Is the First Step in Sexuality Education

The attachment philosophy of child care I have advocated throughout this book is the earliest form of sexuality education. The principles of Christian continuum parenting imply that you are a touching family. Early in your child's life you convey a very special sexual message to him: "We love to *touch you;* you are a special person." This results in a feeling of rightness. It is vitally important that a child feel right about himself or herself as a *person* in order to feel right as a "he" or a "she." If you have modeled touching and loving your child, he is more likely to grow into a touching, loving person. The ability to give and receive affection is one of the greatest gifts you can encourage in your child.

The display of affection between husband and wife is another form of sexuality modeling. Watching Mom and Dad embrace is especially important for the older child. This conveys a feeling of stability within the family in a world where the child sees families breaking apart all around him. Also encourage the show of affection between siblings. Siblings are not usually running over with affection toward each other, and parents usually have to foster an attitude of closeness between them. Love for others is the hallmark of a Christian. Young children cannot see the feeling of love between their parents, but they can see their actions and draw their own conclusions. Become a hugs-and-kisses family.

Basic Principles in Sexuality Education

Genital Awareness

Very early in infancy a child begins the normal and healthy exploration of body parts beginning with thumb sucking and finger play. Genital awareness usually begins sometime in a child's second year, and the initial pulling and poking progresses to awareness of genital sensitivity and the pleasure of self-stimulation. How you react the first time you see your little boy pulling on his penis or your little girl poking into her vagina is probably one of the earliest sexuality messages you convey to your child about his or her genitalia. It is important that a child not perceive his genitalia as "bad." Genitals are part of him or her and should not be called "bad body parts." Genital play does not betray any underlying psychological disturbance any more than thumb sucking does. In fact, a child's ability to use his or her own body parts for self-stimulation is considered by some researchers as evidence of his or her basic security. Children raised in institutions often show less exploration and satisfaction with their own body parts than children raised in the secure home environment.

Your attitude toward toilet training is the next sexuality message you convey to your child. During toilet training, a child develops increased awareness of genital sensation and of the function of his body parts. Your attitude toward toilet training must communicate to your child that what these body parts do is basically good.

Gender Identity

Gender identity is usually understood by age three when children begin to call each other "boys" and "girls." Little girls and boys become aware that they look different and urinate differently. Little girls may wonder where their urine comes from since they do not have penises. Correct this confusion by showing your little girl where the urine comes from, emphasizing that she has the counterpart of a penis so she will not be preoccupied with not having one. Your little boy may wonder why girls do not have penises and he may wonder if he will lose his penis. Proper instruction can certainly minimize this confusion. If you find your child developing confusion and embarrassment, correct this immediately. It is important that this developing sexual person be proud of the body he or she has been given, and it is important that he or she respect the privacy of another person's sexuality. The concept of not touching another child's private areas can be understood by the age of four.

Parents may contribute to genital confusion by using inappropriate terms for genitalia. Not only are these slang terms confusing to your child, but they also convey a subtle message that you are embarrassed about these body parts. The terms *penis, scrotum, vagina,* and *vulva* can be understood by a three year old.

Appropriate gender behavior is usually apparent by age three. Boys are generally more aggressive and enjoy rougher play than girls at this age. How much of this gender behavior is an inborn genetic difference and how much is acquired by parental influence are interesting matters. Certainly, both genetic and cultural influences contribute to early gender identity. It is a known fact that girl infants are gentled more than boy infants. Parents are more likely to roughhouse with boys and play more quietly with girls. In my office, I often fall into this gender trap with my patients by eliciting a hug and a kiss from a little girl and a handshake or a "give me five" from a little boy. I remember my own ridiculous reaction the first time I saw my three-year-old son playing with a doll; fortunately, my wife's wisdom saved the doll from immediately being substituted with a football. These parental-play instincts are probably healthy. In my opinion, unisex attitudes are unhealthy, unchristian, and unscriptural (Eph. 5:22–25). I do believe that programming aggressive behavior in boys may contribute to the much higher incidence of their behavioral problems. The sexes should be gentled equally, and the show of affection and tenderness should be encouraged as equally as the manifestation of assertiveness and physical activity.

It is normal for four-year-old children to shift from one sex role to the other, alternating between dolls and footballs. For some children sex role adaptation is uneasy and prolonged, and they are labeled "tomboys" or "sissies." It is healthy for a child to adapt to his or her sexual role at his or her own pace.

Proper role modeling can help a child seek his appropriate gender behavior. Confusion and dissatisfaction with gender roles is a common cause of sexuality adjustment problems in the older child and adult. Parents, remember you are bringing up someone else's future mate. It isn't fair to leave your child's sexuality education to your son's future wife or to your daughter's future husband.

Young children are quick to perceive the different roles played by mothers and fathers. Although role definitions are less distinct in today's society, I feel it is important to give your children sexual role models. Children often will parent as they were parented. For example, women are likely to breastfeed if they were breastfed. One woman explained why she was still nursing her toddler: "My mother breastfed me until I was two years old."

Women are also more likely to pursue careers outside the home if their mothers did. This trend seems to be balanced by earlier and greater father involvement in infant care. Although the traditional role models of mommies having babies and daddies working are probably foremost in a child's mind, it is important for him to see his father heavily involved in caring for his siblings and his mother. It is unrealistic for a young boy to perceive his father as someone who is always outside the home. One man confided to me, "My image of my father when I was a young boy was getting up in the morning and looking out the window and seeing my father's back and his briefcase as he left for work."

Parents, do not minimize the memories that your child can have of his early sexuality experiences. Most children can remember pleasant experiences from as early as three years of age. What is disturbing is that children can remember often traumatic and unpleasant experiences from an even earlier age.

Where Babies Come From

Sometime around the age of four or five your child may raise the long-anticipated question, "Where do babies come from?" You are now called upon to begin your child's formal sexuality education. The following suggestions will help you begin to teach your child about the miracle of birth.

Expose your child to the births of animals. For example, encourage your child to watch the family pet give birth to her offspring. This is the most natural way to communicate that babies come from inside mommies.

Expose your child to the birth of a sibling. Unfortunately, in our society the mother is usually separated from the rest of her children when she is giving birth. One of the most eye-opening events in our family was the birth of our fifth child, which was attended by all our children, aged four to fifteen. Our four-year-old daughter, who had been prepared and told what to expect, was keenly interested in our family event, and at no time did she seem squeamish or upset. Taking part in and witnessing her mother give birth to her sister certainly conveyed a more realistic view of birth than the usual fairy tales about storks. I strongly encourage parents to allow their children to witness the births of their own brothers and sisters and recommend *Children at Birth* by Marjie Hathaway and Jay Hathaway (Academy Publications, 1978) or *Birth Through Children's Eyes* by Sandra Van Dam Anderson and Penny Simkin (Seattle, WA: Pennypress, 1981) for reading material on this subject.

Watch for openers. Children do not usually ask directly, "Where do babies come from?" They are more likely to give you an opener by looking curiously at a pregnant woman or by showing interest in the new baby a friend's mommy just brought home.

Use correct terms and facts. Babies come from Mommy's uterus, not from her tummy. Use books and visual aids to enhance your instruction but not to substitute it. Suggested books to teach the concept of birth to four to six year olds are *How Babies Are Made* by Andrew C. Andry and Stephen Schepp (Time-Life Books, 1979) and *Being Born* by Sheila Kitzinger (New York: Putnam, 1986). For the older child, do not simply give him a book and ask him to read about sex. Be sure you have read the book yourself to see that both the sexual facts and the sexual *values* meet the standards you have set within your own family. If you do suggest that your child read a certain book, explain why you are suggesting it and invite him to discuss it with you after he has read it.

Give short, simple answers to your child's questions. Give him just as much information as he asks for and satisfy his curiosity at his own pace. Too much detail confuses the young child. Young children think in the concrete, not in the abstract, and are prone to misinterpret statements. *Be sure you understand what your child is asking.* Parents can misinterpret their children's questions easily. This is best illustrated by an old story in which a five-year-old boy asked his daddy at the dinner table, "Daddy, where did I come from?" In response to this dreaded question, both mother and father struggled uncomfortably through a long, involved, and overly anatomical description of the birth process. The five year old, by this time yawning and losing interest, replied, "Johnny next door came from Ohio, and I wanted to know where I came from."

After a child understands that a baby comes from inside Mommy, the next logical question will be, "How did the baby get there?" The age at which children show interest in the details of sexual intercourse varies from four to eight years old. Girls seem to understand the process earlier than boys because they understand what a vagina is. When describing the functions of sperm, egg, testicle, ovary, and uterus, it is best either to draw pictures or use books with simple illustrations. The process of intercourse is one part of sexuality education in which the "solid food is for the mature" advice should prevail. Use wisdom and discretion to teach your child according to his or her level of interest and understanding. Being able to present sexuality to your child comfortably and accurately has the fringe benefit of enabling broad communication with him or her in the future. It conveys to your child that you are an open, accurate, and willing resource of information, and it sets the stage for a more meaningful dialogue by the time your child is a teenager. It is better for children to get proper sexuality education from their parents than to get patchy and often inaccurate information from their peers. Sexuality education is too valuable to be entrusted to the playground.

Dirty Words

Children learn very early that certain words have shock value to adults. Young children often use slang words not because of the meaning these words have but for the reaction they get. A four year old who utters a four-letter word is guaranteed to stop everyone around him in his tracks. Obscene language and swear words are the undesirable part of a child's vocabulary to which he is naturally going to be exposed in his quest for the accepted norms of society. The role of Christian parents is to lay down *beyond any doubt* the accepted norms within the Christian household and to make clear that any language outside those norms absolutely will not be tolerated. This approach implies that parents model for their child language that is acceptable. If a child hears a parent use a "dirty" word or a swear word, then this word falls into the norm. Explain *why* a certain word is not acceptable so your child will understand why it is offensive to you and to others. Using the name of God in vain certainly should not be tolerated within any Christian household, and your child should be taught very early that this commandment is directly from the Lord.

Part 3

Middle Childhood

CHAPTER 6

DISCIPLINE IN MIDDLE CHILDHOOD

So far this book has dealt primarily with the positive aspects of discipline, the instructing and training of your child in the way he should go within his world and toward God. You cannot stop at this, however. You need to know about the next part of discipline—correcting your child if he departs from the way he should go. For corrective discipline to be effective, you must first have the strong foundation of knowing your child, knowing that he feels right, and having Jesus Christ as Lord of your lives.

Also implied in positive discipline is a child's respect for parental authority: "Children, obey your parents in all things, for this is well pleasing to the Lord" (Col. 3:20). A child obeys (the Greek word translated "obey" in the Bible is *hupakouo*, which means "listen to") because she wants to. She obeys (listens to) her parents because she has respect (a reverent fear) for them. Remember, children are resilient and adaptable; children are able to pick up on Christian discipline at any age. If Christian parenting is new to you, openly share your newfound love of Jesus with your child, and she will respond with faith and love.

Having laid this foundation, you may find your child's behavior is desirable most of the time. However, all children have times when they do not go the way they should go and don't always obey (listen to) their parents. This is called a "bent toward evil" by some Christian writers and is mentioned in Proverbs 22:15: "Folly is bound up in the heart of a child." Some children bend more frequently and severely than others, and some children are more difficult to unbend than others, not because of the effectiveness of their parents' discipline but because of the strength of their bent. The behavior modification techniques described earlier do not guarantee the constant "goodness" of your child. They only lower your risk of having to use corrective discipline and increase its effectiveness when you do use it.

This bent toward evil is an important point for Christian parents to consider. It differs from the secular viewpoint toward children, which believes that since children are basically good, they should be left to themselves to determine their direction. Christians believe, however, that unless children are disciplined toward good, they automatically will bend toward evil. I certainly don't believe children should be left to themselves. This approach is contrary to Scripture: "A child left to himself brings shame to his mother" (Prov. 29:15). However, the Christian concept of a child's evil bent also needs some clarification. Humankind (both adult and children) can be viewed as basically good. People are made in the image and likeness of God (Gen. 1:26), and Jesus Christ paid the price for the sin of man. Perhaps this evil bent should be considered as having two causes.

First, every person has some undesirable character traits that often manifest themselves in outward behavior that is not all good. Original sin is present in every person born into the world, as a son or a daughter of Adam and Eve. Pride is the basic sin that caused evil. Strong-willed children are simply demonstrating this pride openly: "I won't give in." When a child is old enough to have a concept of self, he is old enough to be prideful and resistant to parental guidance, and that is what gets him into trouble.

Second, the evil bent in a child may be considered a susceptibility to temptation, a vulnerability. Because the child lacks the wisdom, experience, and discernment of an adult, the child is more vulnerable to temptation, which accounts for part of the evil bent.

Chastening vs. Punishment

Corrective discipline in the Bible is called "chastening" (Prov. 19:18), which differs from punishment. This important distinction separates Christian discipline from secular discipline. Christians follow a different Book. God's way to solve problems and heal relationships is not always the same and not always as easy as man's ways. Many books on discipline list "methods that work" (by "work" they mean methods that stop a certain misdeed), but what works isn't always right in the eyes of God. The Christian approach to solving discipline problems should be perceived by children as so right, so attractive, and so distinctive that they cannot help feeling the value of Christian discipline as a practical way of life.

The terms *chastening* and *punishment* differ in the following ways. *Chastening* implies a redirection of the child toward future, more desirable behavior, performed out of concern and love. It leaves a child feeling right. *Punishment* is retribution, a penalty for a past offense, which may not focus on a redirection toward future, desirable behavior. Punishment may be performed out of anger, without regard for the child's feelings, and does not always leave the child feeling right. Chastening redirects the child along the path he should go; punishment penalizes him for taking the wrong path.

There are three goals in a disciplinary action: (1) to promote desirable behavior, (2) to stop undesirable behavior, and (3) to result in a child's feeling right with himself, his parents, and his God. Punishment alone fulfills only one of these goals—it stops undesirable behavior, at least for the moment. Chastening carries punishment one step further, which is the level that God expects from Christian parents. By giving parents corrective discipline as a parenting tool, God is saying: "Parents, get into your child, find out what is going on inside her, find out why she did what she did, and how she feels as a result of her deed." Give your child the message, "I care and I'm going to mend whatever is causing you to act this way. I love you; I want you to feel right inside."

Perhaps the difference between punishment and chastening can be demonstrated best by a situation in my family. Remember, discipline problems are situation-specific; what applies to one family in one situation may not apply to another family in another situation. One Christmas morning our almost five-year-old daughter, Hayden, was excited as she pranced around dangling a set of sleigh bells. Suddenly our seven year old, Peter, let out a howl of hurt and indignation. His forehead had gotten in the way of Hayden's dangling bells. Peter assumed that Hayden had hit him on the head intentionally, so his howls of protest increased.

Hayden was vaguely aware that something was amiss, that her brother was hurt, and that her mother was giving her "a look," but she felt certain that she hadn't meant to do anything wrong. Martha, my wife, told her to stop swinging the bells around and to see if her brother was all right. She immediately stiffened and resisted her mother's command as Martha pointed out to her that the way she was playing with the bells was not safe when people were nearby because the bells are hard and hurt when they hit a person on the head. She went on, "So please come and tell Peter that you are sorry you hurt him." Hayden shook her head no and got an insulted look on her face, so Martha said, "You still must say you are sorry even if you didn't mean to hurt Peter, and you need to ask him if he is all right. You must care that he is hurting."

Hayden must have felt unjustly accused by my wife's looks and by her brother's howling because she continued to refuse to apologize. We told her she wouldn't be able to open presents until she had made things right with her brother. At this point my wife and I were in agreement on our stand that Hayden had not meant to hurt Peter but she still needed to say she was sorry for hurting him accidentally.

By this time the situation had become a conflict of wills. Hayden's pride was on the line, and she grew more and more resistant to apologizing. Our parental authority was on the line because we had previously been consistent toward expecting and demanding an apology and an "I care" attitude when one of our children hurt another child, whether or not it was accidental. This was also an act of defiance of reasonable parental authority for which a child must be chastened.

Our parental dilemma was how to punish, or rather to chasten, our daughter in this situation. We considered taking her to the bedroom and administering corporal punishment, but we simply did not feel right about this approach. Martha said, "I know her well and something inside her is not right. For one thing she usually does not have any trouble apologizing or forgiving." By now Hayden had gone into a state of near hysterics, crumpling up on the floor and crying out, "No, no, no!" At this point we realized a spanking was not the correct approach at this time. Our anger at her defiance disappeared as we understood we had a frightened little girl on our hands who did not know why she was doing the things she was doing. We sensed that there was more to this than her pride. She was undergoing an internal struggle that she did not understand.

I held her tightly in my arms to control her kicking and flailing, and I explained very calmly but firmly that she was going to have to ask her brother's forgiveness or she would have to sit on the couch and watch while everyone else opened their presents. This calmed her behavior somewhat, but she still refused to comply with our request. I could see that my wife was analyzing Hayden as only an intuitive mother can do. She later confided to me that she was also praying for the wisdom to correct the spiritual turmoil that was making Hayden act in a way that even she was not comfortable with. Martha was thinking of 1 Corinthians 13:4–5: "Love suffers long and is kind; love . . . is not provoked."

We both realized we had to reach Hayden at a deep level. My wife looked her straight in the eyes, and I put my hand on her shoulder. We explained to her that we understood how hard it is sometimes to say you're sorry. Martha told Hayden a story: "When I was a little girl, I refused to apologize to my sister, but my parents didn't know how to help me so I just stayed miserable all day in my pride and anger." We spoke to her in voices of caring authority. Hayden started to calm down and listen, and she soon muttered a tiny "sorry" to her brother. I encouraged her to expand on this apology by looking at him and touching his hand and saying, "I'm sorry, Peter, if I hurt you even though I didn't mean to." Her brother replied, "That's all right." (Always demand that the person apologized to completes the continuum by accepting the apology, thus creating more of a feeling of rightness and justice within the one who is apologizing.)

My wife then said to Hayden, "Now let's pray and ask Jesus to forgive you." She refused, to my surprise, because we have done this before many times. Then I realized she may not have understood why she was to ask Jesus for forgiveness. Actually it was not for the sin of hurting her brother because she hadn't meant to hurt him. We wanted her to pray about her screaming and kicking and defying her parents. So we explained to her, and she accepted that it was the right thing to do, but she said, "You pray for me, Mommy." Martha agreed to pray for her but still told her she would have to pray on her own, because Martha could sense her need for this confession in order to achieve the state of spiritual rightness inside her. I explained to her that as long as she refused to ask Jesus to forgive her she was separated from Him and from the rest of the family:

that it would be as if she were outside the window looking in on us; we were all together but she couldn't be with us. My wife told her that we couldn't force her to say her prayer. But we told her that if she didn't pray and ask Jesus for forgiveness she wouldn't feel good about herself or about her brother and she would not feel close to Jesus at this time. We talked about how we loved her and how Jesus loves her even when she does bad things and He wants to help her. We talked about Jesus' wanting to live in her heart and that maybe she would like to welcome Him because we weren't sure she had ever asked Jesus into her heart in a way she understood. Then she looked at us with big wide eyes, and we knew we had found what she needed.

Early in this discipline dialogue, our other children were observing this conflict, and of course, they made the usual childish snickers as if feeling, "Boy, is she going to get it for defying Mom and Dad," because they knew that defiance is not tolerated in our household. As they saw how we were getting at the root of the problem and their sister was increasingly feeling more right, they began to be more interested and involved in what had become a family situation. At that point we all came together in a circle on the floor where Hayden was sitting and held hands. We prayed for Hayden, praising God for sending His Son, Jesus, to be born and to die for us and to save us from our sins. Also at that time, we took authority over Satan in Jesus' name (something we always do when we sense a spiritual battle). Hayden seemed to sense our firmness and strength in overcoming Satan. She then put her head on Martha's lap and willingly and eagerly repeated a few simple sentences asking Jesus to forgive her for her disobedience. She asked Him to come into her heart, in between quiet little sobs of relief and joy.

Since this incident took place we have grown considerably in our parenting so that now as we look back we would be far less critical of her behavior, less accusatory and less pressuring of her. We have also learned that children sometimes need more time before they are ready and able to say "I'm sorry" and mean it. A child who is angry cannot apologize until the anger has been resolved. And we were still in a punishing mode—that is what we thought of first. Now we would not even consider a spanking.

This soul-searching chastening took about a half-hour; whereas, we could have handled the whole ordeal with a punishment of spanking, which would have taken only a few minutes. If I had picked up Hayden and spanked her for her defiance, I would have accomplished only one thing: perhaps next time she would not be so defiant. I ran the risk of her still refusing to apologize after the spanking, and then what would I have done? Spank harder until she apologized out of fear? This would have left a feeling of not-rightness within the whole family and would have left her feeling a loss of self-esteem and a sense of embarrassment as she reentered the room to join the family. She also would have missed out on a spiritually significant event.

Chastening achieved the desired end—the apology—but it did so by directing her behavior from within, by understanding her and working through her own inner conflict in such a way that the whole family felt right. It made Hayden aware of how her own pride was a stumbling block to Jesus' coming into her heart. It increased her respect for the authority of her parents, who were willing to take control and get to the heart of the matter by showing that "we care and we are going to stick by you; we care enough to give you our very best." It made her more spiritually aware of the forces of good and evil that can overtake a child, but someone older and wiser took charge and led her in the way she should go. This method left every family member feeling right and increased the self-esteem of the offender because she won the battle over herself and temptation. She was a winner in the eyes of her brothers, rather than a loser.

Another benefit of chastening is that it models a kind of discipline for your children to carry over into their own eventual child rearing. Older children observe how their parents discipline the younger children and are very quick to pick up on how their parents discipline under pressure. We learned this when shortly after his encounter with Hayden, we saw our thirteen year old, Bobby, paging through the Bible concordance as if interested in finding a certain topic. I asked Bobby what he was looking up. He replied, "I'm looking up *forgiveness.*"

The Biblical Approach to Spanking

To spank or not to spank is the subject of much emotional debate among child care writers. It has produced controversial books, magazine articles, and TV programs, even legislation. Most (but not all) Christian child-rearing books highly favor spanking as an effective method of discipline. In contrast, Sweden has recently passed a law against spanking. Christian parents are naturally confused about all the mixed messages regarding the subject.

Let me state my opinion of spanking, which is based upon much prayer for wisdom, my own experience as a pediatrician observing what works and what does not, what God says in Scripture regarding discipline, and the opinions of Christian writers whom I respect.

The first point I wish to make is that it is absolutely wrong and against God's design to be mean and abusive toward a child or to strike a child out of frustration, hostility, or anger. The only reason some parents dare do this is that children are small and defenseless.

Second, spanking should not be the first resort in discipline. Parents ought to strive to create such an attitude within their children and an atmosphere within their homes that spanking is unnecessary.

Third, spanking should be reserved for major confrontations when a parent's authority is on the line, situations in which a child willfully defies reasonable authority, and other approaches are not getting through.

In this section on spanking I wish to present not only some clear guidelines based on my own opinion but also some basic scriptural and cultural considerations from which you can evolve your own philosophy on spanking based upon your own individual parent-child situation.

In regard to discipline in general, God has given us some guidelines. We have already discussed the meaning of Proverbs 22:6, "Train up a child." I like to think of the translation "initiate," instead of the word *train,* in connection with giving a child the right start. Discipline begins at birth.

Proverbs 22:15 states, "Foolishness is bound up in the heart of a child." This is sometimes very difficult for parents to understand. However, within the child's nature—as he matures—there is a bent toward good and a bent toward evil. It is up to Christian parents to unbend their child's tendency toward evil. The rest of that verse tells parents what they should do about it: "But the rod of correction will drive it far from him."

The book of Proverbs has more to say about the rod. It is here that the Bible seems to take a clear stand on spanking:

Do not withhold correction from a child,
For if you beat him with a rod, he will not die.
You shall beat him with a rod,
And deliver his soul from hell. (23:13–14)

The rod and rebuke give wisdom,
But a child left to himself brings shame to his mother.
(29:15)

He who spares his rod hates his son,
But he who loves him disciplines him promptly. (13:24)

From the preceding verses it would seem that the Bible takes a clear stand in favor of spanking as the first mode of discipline because of the frequent use of the term *rod* in the Scriptures. I am uncomfortable with this interpretation of these Scriptures for several reasons.

First, while it is clear that the rod does appear to be an object to strike with, the term *rod* is also used in connection with the shepherd's staff: "Your rod and Your staff, they comfort me" (Ps. 23:4). The shepherd's staff was gently used to guide the wandering sheep along the right path. The rod was used to beat off a sheep's predators. This teaching is developed beautifully in the book *A Shepherd Looks at Psalm 23* by Phillip Keller, especially in chapter 8: "Thy Rod and Thy Staff, They Comfort Me." The original Hebrew word *shebet* means "a stick" (for punishing, writing, fighting, ruling, walking). Proverbs 13:24 could be translated: "He who spares his *ruling* [authority] hates his son, but he who loves him disciplines [it doesn't say *punishes*] him promptly." Remember, the book of Proverbs is written in the form of poetry where words often have symbolic meanings. In other Old Testament books there are uses of the word *shebet* that are obviously symbolic.

Second, references to the rod are found primarily in the Old Testament. The Old Testament's basic approach to justice, and probably also to discipline, was different from that of the New Testament. For example, in the New Testament Christ modified the eye-for-an-eye system of justice (Matt. 5:38) with His turn-the-other-cheek teaching (Matt. 5:39–44). In the New Testament, Christ preached gentleness, love, and understanding, as did Paul: "Shall I come to you with a rod, or in love and a spirit of gentleness?" (1 Cor. 4:21).

In the New Testament, Christ did not overturn the laws of the Old Testament but simply fulfilled them to a higher level of spirituality and understanding: He stressed discipline and direction from within the child rather than direction by force from without. Let me suggest that, taken in the context of the total Bible, the total child, and what is known about child psychology and development, spanking is not appropriate. I feel that what God is saying in these Scripture references is simply: Parents, take charge of your child and bring him into submission to your authority. Since the child can be brought into submission just as well (or better) by other means, spanking should not be used. If you take all the rod verses and substitute *parental authority* for *rod*, this would be the true meaning of the verses.

Nowhere in the Bible does it say you must spank your child to be a godly parent.

Reasons for the Anti-spanking Movement

There are three reasons why the anti-spanking philosophy has grown in popularity throughout the past twenty-five years. First, the unwillingness to spank children in the seventies was a natural spin-off from the general movement toward a greater awareness of the feelings and dignity of the child. I feel it is a natural consequence of the childbirth-without-violence philosophy, which has indeed enriched people's regard for the dignity of a newborn as a feeling person. The same feelings that changed child-birthing practices carried over into child-rearing practices. A growing number of parents began practicing concepts similar to those of attachment parenting. To these parents, spanking became synonymous with hurting and violence. Therefore, spanking was naturally foreign to their whole thinking about the parent-child relationship. They became more interested in alternative methods of discipline and were willing to put an enormous amount of energy into those methods. They wanted their children's behavior to be directed by a feeling from within rather than by an external force. Parents who have shied away from spanking for these reasons are to be commended, and as long as they adhere to God's primary message of getting the job done their views about spanking should be respected. If you feel a conflict in your feelings toward spanking, pray and ask God to give you the wisdom to clarify those feelings based upon the preceding Bible passages.

The second reason for the anti-spanking movement, and one with which I have no sympathy, is the carryover from the permissive approach to discipline. A child left to himself will find his own way, according to this approach. The Bible is clearly against this doctrine (Prov. 29:15 and 22:6). A child left to himself will depart from you and will not respect your authority. I feel that parents who do not spank because they follow this general permissive attitude simply show a lack of concern and lazily shirk their responsibility as authority figures. They will be held accountable here on earth for the outcome of their children and after death by the judgment of their Lord.

The third reason spanking is gradually losing favor as a discipline technique is the belief that spanking is the forerunner of child abuse, which has reached epidemic proportions. If a child's behavior is spank-controlled throughout childhood, he is very likely to continue this miserable parenting practice with his own children. Role modeling is an extremely important concept underlying our parenting practices. The role modeling of spanking is indeed a concern. When a child sees you spank another child, or when he himself is spanked, the role-modeling concept he picks up is that it's all right for a big person to hit a little person.

Remember, one of your goals of discipline is to create an attitude within the child and an atmosphere within the home wherein spanking is seldom if ever necessary.

For the most part, children who are the products of attachment parenting are easier to discipline for the following reasons.

1. They love and trust their parents so deeply that they willingly submit to parental authority. They can handle the concept of submission because they

view authority as love and security, not as infringement upon their rights. Consequently, they are less defiant; and defiance is what usually gets children spanked.

2. These children know what behavior is expected of them because their parents have taken the time and energy to convey the behavior they expect as well as the consequences of misbehavior.

3. Because their parents have taken the time and energy to carry out the suggestions for encouraging desirable behavior, the children have less opportunity to deviate into situations that may get them spanked.

4. Children are motivated to please their parents because they have learned there are positive rewards and feedback from their parents when they are pleased—the principle of reinforcement of desirable behavior.

5. Parents depend more on encouragement and discipline rather than on rewards and punishment.

6. Older children who have been reared in this style of parenting are motivated to relate with and please God, their heavenly Father, as they have learned to please in their relationships with their parents.

7. Since children are fun oriented, young children soon learn that their worlds are much smoother and that they actually have more fun when they live according to the rules set by their parents and by God.

The end result is that their parents have achieved the goal of effective discipline—an attitude within their children and an atmosphere within their homes that promote desirable behavior. The children have direction from within themselves. They are motivated toward desirable behavior because they enjoy the right feelings this desirable behavior promotes. They are so accustomed to feeling right that they naturally avoid situations that make them not feel right. They are on their way toward having Christian consciences.

I admit that this level of discipline is not easy to achieve in some children. It takes much more time and energy to create this attitude in your child and this atmosphere in your home than it takes to go to the rod. This is especially true of the strong-willed or high-need child. Disciplining the high-need child is one of the paradoxes of parenting. Most parents who attempt to spank-control their high-need children usually report, "I'm spanking more and getting less results. Spanking seems to be hurting me more than her."

Today's children are generally spanked less than children were years ago. I feel this is a natural consequence of more sensitive parents. For example, suppose you were to ask a parent, "What would you do if your three year old were making an unruly nuisance of himself at a family gathering?" Parent A might respond, "That's simple, I would take him in the other room and redden his bottom; I'll bet he would never act that way again, and it didn't hurt the way I turned out." Parent B might respond, "First, I know that she doesn't settle down in crowds. Second, I would have told my child beforehand what behavior is expected of her. For example: 'We are going to Grandma's house where there will be lots of your cousins to play with. I expect you to play outside, to be careful not to pick up any of Grandma's vases, and to come in when you are called.' And then I would ask my child to repeat what I had said to her." Parent B might also add the reminder:

"I will have to take you into the other room and spank you if you do not do what I ask." (He would carry through on the spanking if necessary and follow the spanking with a sign of love and an explanation of why she was spanked.) Parent C might say, "If he seemed to be getting into trouble, I would first go through my checklist. Is he tired, hungry, bored, etc.? If he 'forgot' after I had reminded him of the rules, I would take him upstairs and help him take a nap, or take him outside for some father-son time together, maybe have a snack. He responds beautifully when I take the time to understand him."

Let me offer an opinion about the approaches taken by Parent A, Parent B, and Parent C. Parent A went directly to spanking as the first resort. I feel he showed lazy parenting, exhibited his power more than his authority, and did nothing to strengthen the respect or love relationship between parent and child. Parents B and C, on the other hand, took time and energy to follow a wiser approach to discipline:

1. They conveyed to the child what behavior was expected of him or her and took the time to be certain that the child understood.
2. They considered the child's needs and feelings and made an effort to channel the child into some play activities that would encourage desirable behavior.
3. If the child showed undesirable behavior, the parents put time and interest into understanding what the feelings and circumstances were that prompted the behavior. They focused on the child rather than on the undesirable actions.
4. Parent B carried out the admonition of spanking if it seemed necessary, but he also followed the

spanking with a sign of love. Parent C is programmed not to spank.

Parents B and C conveyed *both* love and authority to the child. The child knew what behavior was expected of him or her, and the consequences of misbehaving: the result was a greater respect for the authority of his or her parents. Parent B may seem like a last-resort spanker (save your "big guns" till last), which some Christian writers are against (because the child was just waiting for the "big guns" anyway). I don't think so. The big guns won't be needed in most situations. Parent C's approach required the most investment of time and energy—he'll know his child even more.

When You Should Not Spank

There are three times when you absolutely should not spank your child.

1. *Do not spank in anger.* "In your anger do not sin" (Eph. 4:26 NIV). The emotion of anger in itself is not wrong. However, God told people not to allow any of their actions to be motivated by anger. He also said that anger should be justified and short-lived. This admonition applies especially to actions toward children. If you are a parent easily provoked to anger, be on guard against this reaction. Do not spank to release your anger or vent your frustration. Don't wait until you're angry to try to pray. Ask the Holy Spirit to convict you ahead of time about these moments. Develop a stoplight in your emotions that consciously says, "Wait, take time out for a minute, pray, and examine your motives for spanking. Let your hostility settle down." When your thoughts are not clouded by anger, you can usually come up with a more effective means of discipline than spanking. If your primary motive is to avenge your anger, then hold off. Pray for guidance to act according to God's will. "If any of you lacks wisdom, let him ask of God, who gives to all liberally" (James 1:5).

For example, your three year old sits down to breakfast—her mind is full of fantasy, her attention is short, and she is thinking about everything but her food. Oops! There goes her glass of milk all over Mom's clean kitchen floor! You are naturally angry. You just washed that floor. Should you spank? No! This is an example of childish irresponsibility rather than willful defiance. You child did not spill her milk deliberately. This is an accident. Don't be afraid to show that you are angry; children need to know that parents have feelings too. But keep your anger in line with reality. If you explode, you'll have to apologize. Follow your statement of dismay with, "I understand that this was an accident," then add an admonition, "but I expect you to be more careful when you sit at the table." You may also follow with a logical consequence of not refilling her glass of milk if this is a recurrent problem.

Take that same child and the same glass of milk. Suppose you notice the glass of milk is getting closer and closer to the edge of the table. You ask your child to move the glass away from the edge because it may fall and break. (A creative mother shared with me, "I put a large circle on the table with red tape and instructed my child that his glass must stay in the circle.") She defies your admonition and deliberately pushes the glass toward the edge of the table; as you predicted, it falls and breaks. In my opinion, she deserves chastening. This is an act of willful defiance. This testing the limits of authority is a classical childhood ploy. Much more is at stake here than milk spilled on the floor; your God-given authority is at stake. Your child expects to be chastened. What do you accomplish by disciplining her? (1) You impress upon her who is in charge; (2) you show that defiance will always be corrected; and (3) you contribute to the shaping of her future behavior—the more readily she conforms to parental authority, the more readily she will conform to the authority of God in particular and other authority figures in general. Also, she is more likely to follow her own conscience once the appropriate inner authority has been developed.

Here are some alternatives to spanking in this situation. A logical consequence of this on-purpose spilling would be to calmly ask her to help clean up the mess as you talk about what she was feeling—you want to understand and help her understand why she acted that way. Was she feeling angry or jealous (left out) or resentful (crabby inside)? This kind of behavior is a red flag that the child and the family need professional help. A further consequence is that you will assume she does not want any more milk since she pushed it away on purpose. A negative reinforcement could be used here, such as she is now asked to leave the table and sit in a "time out place." If you do this without anger, she will be more likely not to resist. If you are both angry, you will need to cool off so you can help her cool off before proceeding, or whatever you do will be perceived as punishment and no learning will take place. She can come back to the table when she can apologize, and she may need your help doing that. She may need you to pray with her.

2. *Do not spank babies and young children.* In fact, some biblical scholars who have researched the use of the term *rod* in the Scriptures conclude that Solomon was probably referring to the use of the rod for older children, not infants and toddlers. They believe the rod was reserved for particularly wicked deeds and that the child was old enough to understand the meaning of the spankings. I agree with these interpretations, but if you are spanking more and more as your child gets older, then there is a breakdown in your parent-child communication and in your approach to discipline. Professional guidance should be obtained.

3. *Do not spank if you have a weak parent-child relationship.* The principles of attachment parenting are necessary foundations before spanking should ever be considered. Otherwise I feel you are imposing a heavy burden on a fragile foundation which, with continued stress, eventually may lead to a shaky structure (self-esteem) that eventually may crumble. If you have built a solid foundation of love and trust with your child, an occasional swat "to clear the air" will not damage this relationship, but it will not improve it either.

These guidelines for discipline are generalizations. Only when you have gone through the more positive steps for effective discipline and your child still defies reasonable authority would spanking be a consideration. (1) You have followed the principles of attachment parenting, building up a secure love-and-trust relationship; (2) you have clearly defined to your child what behavior you expect of him, and he understands what you expect; (3) you have tried alternative methods to no avail (however, be aware that when you run out of alternative methods, you will usually revert back to the way you were dealt with as a child, no matter how convinced you are that you would never do that. I encourage you to make a lifelong study of discipline and correction [see books listed in the Bibliography] so that you don't spank just because you did not know what else to do); (4) your child willfully defies reasonable authority, and your authority and your relationship with your child are on the line; and (5) you have prayed for guidance for the best method of discipline for your child in a given situation, and your conclusion is that a spanking is in the best interest of your child's inner direction and your authority relationship.

Parents sometimes consider spanking in life-threatening situations. For example, your three to six year old is told not to ride his tricycle into the street. If he does, the tricycle will be put in the garage for one week (logical consequence), and he will be spanked. He rides into the street. This child has neither respect for your authority nor a sense of safety. Parents want to leave an impression on mind and body that will make repeated offenses less likely. Failure to carry through on what you said you were going to do will weaken your future authority relationship and lessen your child's respect for you. An example that is often given is of the child who runs out into the street (life-threatening situation). A child must be taught to respect danger. He must not be left with access to the street until he is old enough to understand. You must be with him, teaching him, until you *know* he is safe. You want him to be able to stop and look both ways before crossing. You also want to have a rule that until he reaches a certain age he must come and ask you first, so you can watch him. You want him to learn to look at the street. You don't want him to learn only to look back at you to see whether you are about to hit him.

How to Develop Spanking "Wisdom"

There are so many variables and so many different parent-child relationships that an absolute dictum of "spank" or "don't spank" is not possible. Here are some general guidelines to help you develop your own attitude about spanking.

1. *Pray for wisdom* to know whether spanking in general is a proper chastening for your child. Disregard all opinions you have heard about spanking lest they cloud your judgment. Open your ears to God's direction, asking Him for an inner sensitivity to spanking in general and in specific circumstances. For our own family, we have concluded, after much prayer, that (1) we will not let unacceptable behavior go unchastened; (2) we are committed to create an attitude within our children and an atmosphere within our home that spanking is not an option; (3) spanking in general is a poor option in all the methods of discipline; and (4) if, in certain circumstances, spanking seems to be the wisest direction, then we are open to using spanking as a form of chastening, not as a punishment. In short, we are programmed against spanking our children. We don't want to spank our children, so we are going to devote a lot of time and energy to utilize alternatives to spanking. This has been a healthy approach for our family. Other parents may choose another viewpoint.

2. *Consider if there are specific risk factors* in your family that affect your attitude toward spanking.

Parents who are most likely *not* to abuse spanking

- have practiced the principles of attachment parenting all along so that they know their children feel right,

- have children whose temperaments are generally easy-going,
- were not spank-controlled as children, and
- are truly walking with the Lord.

Parents who may spank inappropriately

- have generally shaky parent-child relationships,
- were abused as children,
- have high-need children,
- find that spanking does not work,
- are prone to impulsive anger, and
- are not walking with the Lord.

If you have any of these risk factors that might hinder you from spanking appropriately, I suggest you examine your entire parent-child relationship according to the principles already discussed and examine your relationship with God. Some parents simply cannot handle "the rod" wisely. The earlier you accept this and seek help toward alternative means of discipline, the better off your parent-child relationship will be. The product of abusive spanking is anger; the cause of abusive spanking is also anger. An angry child will grow to be an angry adult.

Your child will pick up on your motives for spanking. Are you spanking him for *his* own good or for *your* own good? If you are a parent easily provoked to anger, be on guard. A child spanked in anger will retaliate in anger. This is the main reason parents say, "He's so stubborn; the harder I spank him, the worse he gets."

3. *Spank soon after the offense.* It is important to cool down but a spanking should be given as soon as possible after the offense (Eccl. 8:11) and by the person whose authority is at stake. Don't say, "Wait till your father gets home and then you'll get it."

4. *Help the child accept the spanking.* To help avoid a struggle, explain the whole spanking sequence to your child at a time when she is not just about to have a spanking. You should not have to drag her kicking and screaming off to her "execution." If she resists her spanking, she is also being defiant or else she feels unjustly treated, which means you may need to reexamine your decision.

5. *Explain to your child why you are spanking him.* Some parents may not agree that a child needs to understand why he needs to be chastened. These parents may equate explanations with apologies, which they interpret as weakening their position. But an appropriately administered spanking should not alienate the spanker and the spankee. A wise parent conveys to his child that the spanking is done out of love and out of a God-given duty. "For whom the Lord loves He chastens" (Heb. 12:6) is a good scriptural reference to support your position. Hebrews 12:11 states, "No chastening seems to be joyful for the present, but painful; nevertheless, afterward it yields the peaceable fruit of righteousness to those who have been trained by it." Spanking done as a chastening, not as a punishment, can be effective in some situations. An excellent discussion of the difference between chastening and punishment and how spanking is to be handled if chosen as a form of chastening is found in Jack Fennema's book *Nurturing Children in the Lord* (see Bibliography).

6. *Encourage a confession* (James 5:16; 1 John 1:9). Confession of wrongdoing is very therapeutic. A child is seldom going to welcome a spanking, but understanding and acknowledging he was wrong help him accept the discipline. When a child sees the fairness of a correction, he usually respects the authority figure administering the spanking. Incidentally, he struggles less, which makes spanking easier. "Johnny, did Dad tell you not to ride your bike out into the street? . . . What did you do? . . . You disobeyed me, right? . . . You were wrong, and you could have been hit by a car. . . . You agree that you deserve a spanking?" Johnny will probably manage a few feeble yeses during this interrogation. This little dialogue allows Johnny to feel and release guilt and helps to shape his conscience. This helps him recognize his feelings when he has done wrong and accept a very real fact of life that wrong deeds will be chastened.

7. *Choose a proper instrument for the spanking.* To readers who absolutely disdain any form of spanking, consider the following: I have repeatedly stated in this book that we are programmed against spanking in our family. I have spent most of the discipline chapter teaching parents how to develop alternatives to spanking. Therefore, my position on spanking is clear. However, as a pediatrician for twenty years, I am painfully aware that spanking may lead to child abuse. This section is written primarily to parents who have already made up their minds to spank their child and need guidelines to avoid physical and emotional abuse. There are two schools of thought on what to spank with—a neutral object (a stick, a wooden spoon, etc.) or the hand. Proponents of the neutral object feel that the hand, as part of the parent, is a tool for loving and learning and not an object to be feared. This concept is a carryover from animal behavior psychology. Pet owners are advised never to use the hand to strike with but to use sticks to discipline their pets. Animals shy away from

the objects they are struck with. If you want your dog to fetch your morning paper, don't use a rolled-up paper for discipline or he will learn to hate rolled-up papers.

Some parents associate a stick with "beating" and a hand with spanking; they feel better using their hands. By using your hand you will feel the force of your strength. Other parents feel that if they program themselves away from using their hands to spank, they are less likely to hit their children reflexively out of anger. Having to get the neutral spanking object allows them more time and space to cool off. I am more concerned about the attitude of spanking than the choice of the instrument.

Let me suggest using neither the hand nor a club-like object such as a wooden spoon. A switch is a more appropriate spanking tool. Use a thin, very flexible stick such as a willow branch. The best switch is one that inflicts stinging pain but no injury to the child's bottom. Most cases of child abuse I have seen were inflicted by an angry person behind a heavy hand or a wooden spoon.

Spanking is traditionally administered to the child's buttocks. I feel it is very important to respect the child's sense of modesty and never bare the buttocks. If a child is still in padded diapering, he or she is too young to be spanked anyway. To spank a child anywhere else on his or her anatomy is to risk injury. For example, above the buttocks are located the spine and the kidneys, below are the more bony areas. The face and head must never be struck due to the delicate structures and the emotional insult and trauma that would be caused. A young child's hands never should be spanked because the hands are the tools of exploring.

8. *Follow up after spanking.* An appropriately administered spanking should leave *both parent and child feeling better. An inappropriately administered spanking will leave an angry child and a parent who feels guilty.* To avoid bad feelings all around, follow the spanking with an expression of love. The child may be hesitant to ask for forgiveness or to admit he got what he really should get, and you may not know what to say. Saying "I'm sorry" or "I didn't want to spank you" is confusing to the child. He gets mixed messages: "If you didn't want to spank me, why did you do it?" Or "If you are sorry, then you did something wrong." Of course, if the spanking was done in error, before you had all the facts, you *must* make a sincere apology to your child. Never be afraid to admit you were wrong. This is the best way to teach a child to say *he* is sorry. End a spanking with, "Now let's pray together," after the crying has subsided and you have gathered the repentant child into your arms.

Your prayer should include an expression of love for your child and an acknowledgment of God as your Father and of your accountability to Him for chastening your child out of love. Use Hebrews 12:5–11 for a prayer model after spanking: the prayer for forgiveness and a thanks for forgiveness. During the after-spanking prayer, your child should pick up that you (and God) forgive him. Both you and your child should emerge from a spanking with a clean slate.

Other Methods of Discipline

The Feedback Technique

You should try to understand your child's position before administering any chastening that requires a judgment on your part. Why did your child do what he or she did? Which child started the fight? As has been said before, you can control your children's actions, but you cannot control the feelings that prompted these actions.

One of the ways of learning about these feelings in your child is called the "feedback technique." In this technique, a parent in the position of authority conveys the message, "I care." He then carefully listens to the child and discerns what the child is feeling or trying to express. Then he feeds back to the child what he thinks the child felt. For example, your frustrated three year old throws a toy at her brother. She is angry, losing control, and she needs understanding and support, in addition to chastening, for her actions. Begin by formulating in your own mind what she is feeling and then say to her, "You are angry and this is why you hit your brother. . . . I understand. . . ." The feedback technique is even useful for your toddler whose ability to understand words and concepts usually is more advanced than her ability to speak. Your toddler may not be able to express her feelings verbally, but she will usually be able to understand your verbal expression of her feelings. This technique is also effective for the older child or adolescent who does not like to listen to your opinion of her behavior until she feels you truly sympathize with her feelings. Nothing is more frustrating to a teenager than a parent's long tirade or reprimand before the parent attempts to understand her position. When you begin your discipline methods with the feedback messages of "I care," "I understand," you help your child be more willing to accept your authority and your advice. (See the Faber and Mazlish book, *How to Talk So*

Kids Will Listen and Listen So Kids Will Talk, listed in the Bibliography.)

Natural and Logical Consequences

Understand natural and logical consequences. The principle of consequences for misbehavior is one of the oldest biblical forms of corrective discipline. Natural consequences are a form of corrective discipline in which the punishment is automatically built into the act. For example, a child touches a hot stove and gets burned; you can be sure he will not touch that stove again. Psalm 7:15–16 is a good biblical example of natural and logical consequences for an adult.

> *He made a pit and dug it out,*
> *and has fallen into the ditch which he made.*
> *His trouble shall return upon his own head,*
> *And his violent dealing shall come down on his own*
> *crown.*

Logical consequences are a form of corrective discipline in which the person in authority, usually a parent, makes a rule and clearly points out the consequences for breaking this rule. The implication in this discipline is that if a child chooses to break the rule, he also chooses the consequences. If you see your child heading for the wrong path, you can point out to him, "You are making a poor choice," letting him realize his responsibility for his own actions and giving him a chance to reconsider before the consequence is actually upon him. In this form of discipline the "punishment" closely fits the misdeed. God frequently used logical consequences in the Old Testament, such as the law of restitution: if a man stole a sheep or killed it, he replaced it with four sheep. Sports utilizes logical consequences. A football team plays according to the rules, and the penalty for breaking the rules is agreed upon before-hand.

Withdrawing privileges is a form of logical conse-quences. The most classical biblical example of this is Adam and Eve. They disobeyed the rules of the garden, and God took away their garden.

Logical consequences is a very effective form of discipline for older children, especially in large families, in order to get the busy household running more smoothly. For example, "Your bike is to be put on the porch every evening after you are finished riding it. If you forget, the bike will be put in the garage for one week."

The Family Council

The family council is a form of corrective discipline that is a must for large families and is an effective way to use logical consequences. In our family, one of the ways we use the family council is to sort out problems. In a large family everyone must have certain responsibili-ties, and with maturity come increasing privileges and a proportional increase in responsibilities. Every so often when the list of "I forgots" gets too long and our household regresses from busy order to ordered chaos to disordered chaos, I call the troops together around the dining room table for a family council. I list the behaviors and responsibilities expected of them and make sure each child understands the list. I then convey to each child the consequence of not doing the jobs or of continuing certain undesirable behaviors. For exam-ple, anyone who grumbles puts a dime in the "grumble box," or gets an extra job; any teen who habitually dawdles in the morning and is not ready when the carpool driver arrives either walks to school or misses school that day (which also has its consequences); the car cannot be used until it is cleaned out; and if toys are not put away according to the rules, they get put up for a week.

Disciplining the High-Need Child

In some respects, all children are strong-willed but some have stronger wills than others and I call them "high-need" children. Because parenting these high-need children can be a very complicated subject (see *The Fussy Baby* in Bibliography), I will attempt to help you understand why your child has high needs and why the usual techniques or methods apparently don't work.

The high-need child is impulsive. He has great difficulty saying no to himself and even more difficulty saying yes to you. He is driven. The high-need child very often has higher than average intelligence. He is not satisfied with average teaching or learning. In short, an above-average child requires above-average parenting. He will require above-average teaching at school, and he requires above-average teaching about God at home.

Parents, take heart. There is light at the end of the tunnel. In parenting, there is what I call the "investment-return ratio." In all children, the more parental energy invested, and the earlier and more consistently it is invested, the greater are the returns. For the high-need child, the investment-return ratio is even greater; more needs to be invested but more is returned.

If a bank had an investment plan for a high-need child, the manager would say to you, "Your child will need an above-average college. You will need to invest more, invest earlier, invest more consistently, and invest for a longer time. You will be tired from working extra hours. The dividends will be slow in coming and may not arrive for a long time. You may not always be aware that it is paying off. The investment has a greater risk because if it is not kept consistently high, the value of the stock will fall more sharply. However, if it is kept up, your rewards will be beyond all expectations." These creative children, if properly parented and prayed for, usually turn out to be a great joy to their parents and to God.

You will need to show more love and apply careful correction to your high-need child. Each parent must work out the proper ratio of behavior modification to correction. On the surface it may appear that the high-need child needs more correction and less behavior modification, but for most high-need children, the opposite is true. This concept is best illustrated by a situation I had in my office when counseling the parents of high-need two-and-a-half-year-old Johnny. Johnny had been an energy-draining baby who demanded constant motion and physical contact in order to be settled, and even that did not always work. After two and a half years, the parents were worn out. Unfortunately, Johnny arrived at a time when his father was very busy trying to get ahead by working longer hours. As Johnny demanded more, his mother gave more, and his father managed to escape from the entire situation by working longer hours. The situation deteriorated into a high-need child who did not feel right, a tired mother who also did not feel right, and a father who became more successful in his corporation than in fathering his child.

One day the father said to me, "You know, I'm spanking Johnny more and more, but I'm just not getting through to him." I then asked the father, "Are there times when you notice you don't have to spank Johnny as much?" The intuitive mother quickly volunteered, "On days when he and Johnny have a lot of one-on-one fun time together, Johnny is the most wonderful child." In discussing this situation further I discovered that both parents, who were themselves labeled by their parents as strong-willed, were gifted children and turned out to be high achievers. They completed the strong-willed continuum by producing their own strong-willed (high-need) child. It's interesting that heredity often does play a factor, which supports my feelings that many high-need children do not have behavioral problems but are instead intelligent, gifted children who need high-input parenting. I advised these parents to put the rod to rest for the time being, discussed the need-level concept with them, and advised the father to redirect his priorities.

The high-need child's impulsiveness is usually what gets him in trouble. Impulse control is very hard for the high-need child and for his parents because, as has been stated, these children have such high need levels. I do not mean that their high needs can be satisfied by material things. These children need focused attention from their parents, a lot of touching and gentling, a lot of playing with, building with, reading with, talking with. A high-need child needs to learn that she can't have every toy she sees or every ice-cream cone she wants. She needs to be put in her place if she is hurting another person in some way, such as biting or scratching. The control of aggressive behavior and of the "I wannas" is much easier for parents if they have practiced selective gratification early in the child's life. In an increasingly materialistic world of instant turn-ons and instant entertainment, impulse control is a high-priority objective for parents of all children, but especially of high-need children.

Discipline challenges continue throughout childhood. In the next chapter we will take a closer look at the role of spiritual training in disciplining the six- to ten-year-old child.

CHAPTER 7

DISCIPLINING THE CHILD SIX TO TEN YEARS OLD

During the first five years of your child's life, you should create a total Christian home so the following values are instilled in him or her.

- God is important to Mom and Dad.
- God seems to enter into everything we do as a family.
- God loves me; I am a special person in God's sight.
- God disciplines me through my parents when I do wrong.
- I feel right when I act right, and I do not feel right when I act wrong (the beginning of conscience).
- I fear God (in the sense of awed respect for God).

From this foundation, he can develop the primary goals of middle childhood: to increase his self-esteem and to accept your Christian values as his own Christian values.

Between ages six and ten your child will either accept and develop your Christian values or question them and evaluate alternative value systems. How much of your Christian values he accepts or rejects depends on two variables: (1) the depth and consistency of Christian teaching in your home and (2) how susceptible your child is to competitive value systems. From this, it follows that your main objective during this state is to saturate his environment with Christian values that enhance rather than weaken the values you instilled in him during his earlier years. The next objective is to protect him from those outside influences that compete with and may seriously weaken the Christian values taught at home. Although your child may live in a strong Christian home, he is not exposed to a totally Christian world. The big secular world out there often fails to steer him in the way he should go.

Your central focus is to emphasize the factors that help your child grow internally toward his or her commitment to a Christ-centered life. You can achieve this by continuing to model strong spiritual principles—the concepts of God, family devotions, daily prayer, prayable situations, and teachable moments—and by continuing to carry out Christian principles of discipline discussed earlier. Continuing to provide this spiritual home model for your child gives him a strong outer protective shield that wards off attacks from competitive value systems.

Teach your child to put on the protective armor of Christ (Eph. 6:13–17). A young child's armor is very thin, like a semipermeable membrane that is unable to filter selectively those things that add to or take away from her spiritual growth. Strong and consistent home spiritual training helps the child strengthen her protective armor.

Your values are in direct contrast to non-Christian

philosophies that encourage parents to expose their children to all the influences of the "real world" and to let them make their own decisions. I strongly oppose this approach. A young child does not have the wisdom and discernment to be able to follow those things that are of God and turn from those that are not of God. A child left to himself is in trouble (Prov. 29:15).

Think of the instruction and protection a child receives when participating in Little League sports. In these activities the child undergoes proper coaching that builds strength from within. The child is equipped with protective clothing and is allowed to compete only with players of his or her own age and weight in order to reduce the likelihood of physical injury. Parents should do even more to instruct and protect their children in regard to influences that cause spiritual injury.

Getting to Know the Other People in Your Child's Life

As your child grows into a social person, he becomes involved in many activities outside the home. He is confronted by a wide variety of value systems from other authority figures. They are called "persons of significance," and they include teachers, coaches, pastors, scout leaders, so on. Before you entrust your child to the authority of any of these persons, be sure you have a clear understanding of their personal values and of what they will be teaching your child. Impress upon these persons the values you wish your child to be taught.

One of the strongest influences on a child more than five years old is her peers. She depends on them for acceptance. This is one of the strongest arguments for the wisdom of home schooling. During this peer-dependency period a child senses the norms of the children she knows, and she begins to accept or reject those values. Children, especially those younger than six or seven, do not have the wisdom and discernment to make a judgment about the peer values that run contrary to those of her parents. Faced with a choice, she may turn her back on the values taught by her parents. Parents often have less control over the effects of peer pressure than they do over the influences from older persons of significance. Although it is no guarantee, it helps to know the values of the parents of your child's peers before encouraging their friendships.

You may protest, "But, Doctor, isn't this causing my child to lead a sheltered life?" Yes, it is. I feel God is very clear in His directive (Deut. 6:7–9) that parents should instill Christian values into their children so deeply that they develop the wisdom and discernment to reject competitive value systems. Until the child has reached the age when he has these abilities, parents should shelter him from, or rather filter out, any person or activity that endangers his spiritual growth. There is no benefit in thrusting the young child out among the thorns of the world until he is able to protect himself. Parents never can protect their children fully from competing influences, of course, but they certainly can minimize them. Many times you will be called upon to turn a spiritually dangerous situation into a teachable situation.

When your child is confused by a competing value system, seize the opportunity to explain why what the other person said or did is not in accordance with God's plan. After you have explained this fully to your child, ask her the leading question, "How do you feel about this? Would you feel right or wrong if you did . . . ?" Encouraging your child to express his judgment about an alternative value system is one of the ways you can take a running inventory of how he is accepting your value system.

Helping Your Child Build Self-Esteem

In keeping with the idea that the child who feels right acts right, you should help your child build his self-esteem during this stage. In the first few years of life a child's self-esteem is determined primarily by how he feels his parents feel about him, but in middle childhood his self-esteem is determined primarily by how he feels others feel about him. Dr. James Dobson in his book *Hide or Seek* (see Bibliography) has emphasized the important fact that physical attractiveness is one of the prime determinants of a child's self-esteem in today's society. Abilities in sports and in academics are the next yardsticks by which a child's self-worth is measured. A child who is considered the ugly duckling of the crowd, is uncoordinated in sports, and is not a whiz at academics is going to be troubled. The older child can take some consolation in the realization that he is loved by God, but the child at this age level is deeply affected by where he fits into his peer group.

If you have a child who is not obviously blessed with one or more of these "measures" of success, you should help him become involved in some activity in which he can succeed and gain recognition. Involvement and recognized success are vital to self-esteem development at this stage. Your ability to know him in the early years of his development really pays dividends now. Parents who truly know their children know their strong points and weak points; therefore, they are more able to create environments that allow their strong points to flourish, and they can protect them against attacks on their weak points. Whether it is sports, music, academics, gymnastics, or crafts, it is vital for every child to receive recognition that he is good at something. If you have difficulty recognizing what your child is good at, here is a tip: children are most likely to be interested in what they are most comfortable doing. Allow a child to pursue and develop her own interests; do not force her to excel in something you are interested in. If your child succeeds at something and receives recognition for her success, her self-esteem is so boosted that it is likely to carry over into success in other fields.

Let me suggest a social aid that is particularly useful for the shy child who has difficulty winning friends. Encourage your child to invite friends over to your home. Create an atmosphere that makes him feel comfortable bringing another child home to play and to stay overnight. His home becomes his castle. He is king of the hill automatically. He is more likely to play a better game if the game is played in his own ball park.

The Christian Edge

The incidence of problems with low self-esteem seems to be increasing in children, especially during the ages of preadolescence and adolescence. I believe one of the main reasons for this epidemic is that today's children are constantly being bombarded with the importance of physical attractiveness, athletic skills, and academic aptitudes. They are struggling constantly for acceptance in these three areas, and if they don't achieve it, they are really in trouble. Today a child has many more choices of direction and many more relationships outside the home that will either accept or reject him. In the past, the extended family was a child's primary relationship until he was ready to leave home toward the end of his teens. There was no doubt that he was strongly loved by nearly everyone around him. As parents seem to be giving up more and more of their responsibilities to institutions outside the home, children are required to measure up to more and more relationships outside the home, which I feel is the basis for the current diseases of low self-esteem.

Christian families have an edge in overcoming this self-esteem problem in children. If you rear your child in a Christ-centered family and strive to develop the inner circle of Christian commitment as described here, your Christian child can feel the constant love of God. Parents, drive home to your children the fact that Christ loves them; He gave up His life for them. This is a very difficult concept to convey because children are more influenced by the concrete relationships they see on earth, and God is still an abstraction to many children. However, the child between six and ten years of age can achieve this inner awareness of the love of God. Your child's acceptance of Jesus as his or her personal Savior will be the most lasting preventive medicine against diseases of low self-esteem. Most of the peer relationships a child will form throughout his life will be temporary and fleeting; the love relationship a child has with his parents and with his God will be a lasting relationship.

Helping Your Child Develop a Christian Conscience

Usually children younger than six are unable to discern right from wrong by the reasoning process. The young child learns what is right or wrong by the response he gets from a certain action. If he gets a desirable or pleasurable response to a certain action, such as when he obeys his parents, he is likely to continue this "right" behavior. If he gets an undesirable or even painful response from an action, he is less likely to repeat this "wrong" action. Because preschool children lack the insight into the basic rightness or wrongness of an action, it is very frustrating to try to reason with them. As a result, corrective discipline in the preschool child is usually in the form of chastening, consequences, or correction. As a child becomes older (usually around six years of age) he is more able to reason and, therefore, more able to be reasoned with. Parental discipline gradually shifts from the corrective measures of consequences and correction to the more guiding measures of counseling.

Ephesians 6:4 is the key verse for this focus on discipline methods. Let's look at this verse in three different translations:

Fathers, do not exasperate your children; instead, bring them up in the training and instruction of the Lord. (NIV)

And you, fathers, do not provoke your children to wrath, but bring them up in the training and admonition of the Lord. (NKJV)

And now a word to you parents. Don't keep on scolding and nagging your children, making them angry and resentful. Rather, bring them up with the loving discipline the Lord himself approves, with suggestions and godly advice. (TLB)

Paul summarized the entire parent-child discipline relationship in his epistle to the Ephesians:

Children, obey your parents in the Lord, for this is right. [Paul carried his thought a step further in Col. 3:20: *Children, obey your parents in all things, for this is well pleasing to the Lord.*] *"Honor your father and mother,"* which is the first commandment with promise: *"that it may be well with you and you may live long on the earth."* And you, fathers, do not provoke your children to wrath, but bring them up in the training and admonition of the Lord.* (6:1–4)

This scriptural passage says it all about discipline, especially discipline of the school-age child. Carefully analyze it to determine exactly the relationship God expects between parent and child.

"Children, obey your parents." This is a natural law between parents and their offspring. "In the Lord." Here God raised this natural law of obedience to a Christian level. Parents are God's representatives (their authority is from Him in the chain of command) so that a child's obeying his parents implies obedience to God and fear, or awed respect, of the Lord. You have learned earlier that how a child learns to obey and respect his parents at an early age often determines how he learns to obey and respect God at a later age. This probably presupposes that the child is walking with the

Lord as much as possible at his particular age and level of understanding. "For this is right" ties in to the feeling of rightness I describe repeatedly throughout this book, a feeling a child receives when he is walking with his parents according to God's design for the parent-child relationship and walking with the Lord according to the commandments of the Lord.

"Honor your father and mother." Commentators on this verse feel God purposely used the word *honor* instead of *love* to elevate the significance of this commandment. The term *honor* implies love, respect, and obedience. "Which is the first commandment with promise." In the rest of the Ten Commandments God gave simple statements but did not attach any promise or reward if people keep the commandments. Here, Paul referred to the fact that God attached a promise to this commandment, and the promise is "that it may be well with you and you may live long on the earth." The fact that God made this promise to children who honor their fathers and mothers elevates the importance of the commandment. As I was reading this verse an awe-inspiring idea occurred to me: although this commandment is given directly to children, we can infer from this that parents must be honorable, and also be spiritual models for their children. If you fail to give your children models to honor, are you not also robbing them of the promise that God has given them for honoring their parents?

Paul completed this continuum of parent-child discipline by advising parents, especially fathers, to merit honor from their children: "And you, fathers, do not provoke your children to wrath." God here advised fathers not to be so unjust and harsh with their children that they cannot honor their parents and cannot obey their authority. Instead of angering or exasperating their children, fathers are advised to bring them up "in the training and admonition of the Lord." This sums up the Christian discipline God expects you to give your children. *Training* implies both instructive and corrective discipline, the two main forms of discipline we discussed in the discipline of the preschool child. *Admonition* implies counseling and is derived from the Greek word which means, "training by word of encouragement, a reproof for the purpose of improvement." The last phrase of this verse, "of the Lord," is usually interpreted to mean such discipline and admonition that the Lord would exercise on His children.

Parents, use Ephesians 6:1–4 as your model for discipline. These verses are full of suggestions and insight into the parent-child relationship. Meditate on them and study them.

As your child becomes older and develops more insight for his or her actions, your discipline will shift from corrective discipline to admonition or counseling, although there is usually need for both instructive and corrective discipline at all ages. The elements in counseling the older child are similar to those mentioned earlier for chastening the younger child: confrontation, acceptance, confession, and healing or covenanting.

1. *Confrontation.* When your child does a certain undesirable action which, in your judgment, is not in accordance with the Christian values in your home, confront him or her with the action. A model for confrontation is given in Matthew 18:15, "If your brother sins against you, go and tell him his fault between you and him alone." It is in the confrontation part of counseling that a Christian parent has the edge. Only a parent who is honored by his child is truly able to counsel his child. Confrontation from the honored parent toward the obedient child is also done in a position of genuine love for that child. The love must flow from the parent during the confrontation and be felt by the child who receives the counsel. A confrontation done out of love should strengthen the child-parent relationship rather than weaken it. Christian confrontation means more than exposing the offender's deeds; it implies discerning his spiritual needs and restoring the offender.

2. *Acceptance.* After you confront your child in love, help him accept the confrontation. The older he becomes, the less willing he may be to accept confrontations. He may see them as direct attacks on his need for independence. If you have previously laid the foundation of respect for your parental authority and have given your child the "I care" message in the initial confrontation, your child may be more open to accept your counsel. One of the most frustrating situations in counseling your child is his tuning you out; he may be standing next to you, but his mind and spirit are somewhere else. If this happens, you may need to add physical touching (put your arm around his shoulder) and insist on eye-to-eye contact as you are talking to him.

3. *Confession.* Confrontation and acceptance should be followed by your child's confession of his wrongdoing. If your child feels threatened or regards confessing as a weakness, pray with him about the following scriptural passages, reminding him what Scripture says about confession: "If we say that we have no sin, we deceive ourselves, and the truth is not in us. If we confess our sins, He is faithful and just to forgive us our sins and to cleanse us from all unrighteous-

ness"(1 John 1:8–9). James 5:16 reminds your child of the healing property of confession: "Confess your trespasses to one another, and pray for one another, that you may be healed. The effective, fervent prayer of a righteous man avails much." Proverbs 28:13 is a warning for those who do not confess: "He who covers his sins will not prosper, / But whoever confesses and forsakes them will have mercy."

Confession is one of the earliest helps toward conscience building. In order for your child to confess that he has done wrong, he must first make a value judgment that his action was indeed wrong. A child's conscience is like an internal computer, and each value judgment of right or wrong becomes a bit of information stored into his computer for later retrieval. If a parent lets wrongdoing go uncounseled, the child is deprived of a bit of information to store in his conscience. Each act of biblical counseling is stored in the child's memory for later retrieval. I am not suggesting that you confront your child for every little offense, for sooner or later the overcounseled child will turn off his receiver. If each act of counseling carries with it the "I care for you, my child" message, this tuning out is unlikely to happen. For the child "who always seems to be in trouble," biblical counseling will give the message that his parents will never give up on him.

Listen to your child. Don't be too quick to judge the rightness or wrongness of an action before you understand his position. The older the child, the more sensitive he is to attacks on his own position. Nothing frustrates a teenager more than the feeling that his counselor does not genuinely understand his position. A child does not expect his parents to agree with his position, but he does expect them to listen. The Bible gives us clear counseling about the importance of listening: "He who answers a matter before he hears it, / It is folly and shame to him" (Prov. 18:13). James 1:19 is good counsel for parents about judging too quickly: "Let every man be swift to hear, slow to speak, slow to wrath."

4. *Covenanting.* The final step in the counseling process is covenanting, which implies a commitment on the part of the child not to repeat the wrong action and a commitment on the part of the parents to stand by the child to help him redirect future behavior.

Our son Peter is usually a well-disciplined child, for which we continually praise the Lord. One day, however, he lost his patience and in a defiant tone of voice yelled at his mother in one of those "I won't do it" situations. I immediately stepped in and took charge by calmly but firmly taking Peter by the arm, looking him squarely in the eye, and confronting him by saying, "Peter, you have lost control of yourself. I will not tolerate your talking to your mother that way for two reasons; she is your mother and I love you. Come on outside; we need to have a little talk about this."

I next elicited an acceptance and confession from Peter that he was wrong in showing this outburst of disrespect for his mother. In order to make a spiritual lesson out of this counseling, I brought in the commandment of "honor your mother" and discussed the meaning of the term *honor.* During the acceptance and confession of this wrongdoing, I brought out some of Peter's feelings that prompted his action. "Peter, why did you speak to your mother that way, and how did you feel about it after you lost your temper?" Peter then defended his position by pleading his case that he felt what his mother was asking him to do was unfair.

I listened to Peter as he defended his position, and the more he talked, the more he began to realize he was indeed wrong. But he was still a bit uneasy about outwardly admitting it. While a child is struggling for a confession, it is important to convey a sensitive understanding of his position without being manipulated into agreeing with him.

Following the confession and acceptance that he was wrong, we made a covenant, "The next time you feel like being disrespectful to your mother, I want you to think immediately about what we talked about today. If it helps, go into another room where it is quiet and ask God to help you control your temper. Now, Peter, I am going to say something very important to you and I want you to understand it. I absolutely will not tolerate your shouting at your mother, and I am going to do whatever it takes to keep you from doing this. Do you understand me, Peter?" (Allow ample time for your child's response, and if you are not getting it, repeat your admonitions until he does respond.) "I am going to help you help yourself, Peter. God has given you to me, and some day I am going to have to answer to Him for how I disciplined you. I am going to keep riding hard on you when I see you losing your cool, Peter, because I love you, and I am your father." (You may bring in Heb. 12:6, "For whom the LORD loves He chastens.") "Now let's pray together and then go tell Mommy you are sorry for shouting at her." This episode ended with Peter's apologizing in the accepting arms of his mother.

A child's conscience is her inner policeman which tells her what she ought to do and what she ought *not* to do. One of your prime goals as a Christian parent is helping your child build a Christian conscience. Christian parents are evangelists in their own homes, proclaiming the gospel to their children and instilling into them a clear understanding of right and wrong based on both common sense and God's love. When their children are old enough to walk in faith, they should carry with them the inner voices of their teachings that will continue to direct them in the way they should go.

During the last few years of your parenting, the following fundamentals lay the foundation for the development of the Christian conscience, which begins sometime around the age of six.

1. Follow the early principles of Christian continuum parenting, which lead to a feeling of rightness within the child.
2. Develop the methods of effective Christian discipline, especially the positive reinforcement of desirable behavior and negative reinforcement of undesirable behavior.
3. Constantly encourage impulse control.
4. Use chastisement as your primary method of corrective discipline.
5. Give your child a clear understanding of what is right and what is wrong by counseling him and by deepening his knowledge of Scripture.

The imprint you have made upon your child during her early formative years now becomes a part of her. It is as if she takes you with her as she ventures into the world. After you have laid this foundation, you can build her conscience primarily by reinforcing all of the principles mentioned here as long as she remains under your influence. I cannot overemphasize the importance of keeping constant vigilance over your child in order to help her develop impulse control and in order to counsel her through undesirable behaviors.

In my opinion much of the literature of child psychology goes overboard in sacrificing principles of good discipline simply to avoid making the child feel "guilty." I do not share this philosophy. Throughout this book I have stressed that a child who feels right, acts right, and vice versa. If a child acts wrong, he needs to feel wrong. If he acts contrary to the commandments of either his parents or God, some little voice inside ought to say, "You should not have done that." As a result of this voice of conscience, the child does not feel right (in other words, he feels guilty). A child who is accustomed to an internal feeling of rightness does not like to feel wrong, and this feeling of guilt is an extra incentive for him not to repeat the actions that make him feel wrong. There is too much concern that guilt will damage a child's self-esteem. On the contrary, guilt feelings, if properly handled, actually can boost a child's self-esteem because these feelings serve to keep future behavior in check. However, excessive guilt is not part of God's design and needs to be dealt with and healed through Christian counseling.

At this point I would like to offer a word of encouragement to parents who are hurting because they feel that their child is in trouble and is not developing a conscience. Don't give up; hang tough. Every time your child goes off the track, pick him up and put him back on it. As I mentioned earlier, every time a child's undesirable action is redirected by a person whose authority is respected, you are moving one step closer to helping him develop his own discipline from within.

My dear Christian parents, an unfortunate reality is that many obstacles in the world compete with your child's conscience. It seems that God foresaw the difficulty parents would have in competing with these alternatives, and He promised you help through the Holy Spirit. Parents, daily ask God to fill your child with the Spirit, which is the ultimate directive of a Christian conscience. First Corinthians 2:15 states that the spiritual man (meaning the Spirit-filled man) makes judgments about all things. He has spiritual discernment or a Spirit-directed conscience.

Teaching Your Child to Be a Servant

John 13:4–17 tells the story of Jesus' washing His disciples' feet. Verses 14 and 15 state, "If I then, your Lord and Teacher, have washed your feet, you also ought to wash one another's feet. For I have given you an example, that you should do as I have done to you." This is explicit instruction from the Lord that Christians must learn to serve one another. The best way for this ministry of service to become part of a Christ-centered life is for it to begin at home. Of course, children experience the way they are served by their parents, and your attitude ought to be one of serving. But children need to learn it for themselves in the way they can care for one another and for older people in the family, parents and grandparents. Job lists can be presented in this way to bring a spiritual dimension to daily chores. Special needs of family members can be great opportunities for service—push great-grandmother in her wheelchair; spend time keeping baby amused so Mom can relax; make brother's bed to surprise him; and so on. The possibilities are endless, and so are the blessings.

CHAPTER 8

CHRISTIAN SCHOOLS

"When should my child start school?" is a common question parents ask. There are many studies on childhood education which yield conflicting advice, leaving parents who want the best for their children to flounder in a sea of uncertainty. In today's educated society, the school you choose for your child is a major influence on his or her self-esteem. Therefore, where and when to send your child to school are decisions that should be made with much prayer and consultation. I am not a professional educator, but as a pediatrician I see children daily who have been positively or negatively affected by their school experiences, and I will share with you what I have learned from my observations.

When to Send Your Child to School

When deciding if your child is ready for school, ask yourself, "How will school contribute to my child's self-esteem?" Parents should program themselves to consider the effect of school on their children's self-esteem first and on their academic performance second. This may sound like heresy and a reversal of priorities to some parents who make education a top priority in their child's life. As a Christian father of eight children, I too make education a top priority, but I am much more concerned about how my children feel about themselves as individuals than about how they feel about themselves as students. I have observed that a child who feels good about himself or herself as a *person* has a much greater chance of performing well academically. On the other hand, a child with a low self-esteem is less likely to do well in school. In my experience, low self-esteem contributes more to learning problems than specific learning disabilities do.

■ Selecting a Preschool: Why? When? Where?

By the age of three, most children show a strong desire for companionship as well as a desire to refine the skills they have thus far acquired. Preschools serve both these desires. Whether your child's needs during this stage can be met more effectively at home or at a preschool depends primarily upon your child and your family situation. There are a few points you can consider when deciding.

Parents are still the most effective teachers. Preschool education begins at home, and an outside facility should add to and complement the home education, not be a substitute for it. You may, therefore, initially wish to send your child only a few hours each week and let her extend her time at preschool at her own pace.

The preschool should be an extension of the home. The facility you select should have the same child-rearing values and priorities as you. Ask advice about various preschools in your area from other parents who share your principles of child rearing. Parents sharing the same values of child rearing have been responsible for the "co-op preschools" (parents take turns staffing the school). What the co-op may lack in structure and organization, it makes up for with high parental involvement.

Visit the preschool for a preview. The four major aspects you should consider are the teachers, the equipment, the curriculum, and the child interaction.

Call ahead to find out the best time to visit. Surprise visits have mixed benefits. For a variety of reasons it may not be a truly representative day, or the director and particular teacher may not be available if you arrive unannounced. Take your child along. You will get different reactions from your child at the various schools. Mothers are especially intuitive about their child's positive or negative feelings.

Discuss the general philosophies of the school with the director and observe the specific qualities of the teacher who will be working most closely with your child. Is she basically a kind and nurturing person who knows how to get children excited about learning? Is she someone your child will enjoy being around? How does she handle apparent misbehavior? Does the child get the needed support when he is apparently failing in effort? Are the groups small (maximum of ten per teacher)? Are the children really enjoying themselves and interacting? Are they smiling? Do the children's creations decorate the walls? No matter how crude a child's creations may be, are they praised and respected? Are the snacks nutritious? (All preschoolers should have mid-morning and mid-afternoon snacks because of children's tendencies to low blood sugar following prolonged activity.) Is there alternating active and quiet play, so necessary for this age? Examine the outside play equipment. Is it safe and well planned? For example, climbing equipment is generally safer and more instructive than swings. In addition to checking the climbing equipment, which teaches gross motor development, examine the arts and crafts equipment for fine motor development. Are children taught that everything has a place? This encourages a sense of order. Are they encouraged to "mess a bit" in something such as finger painting? If you are big on "preparedness for school" then you will want to examine the preschool's methods of reading and writing preparation, their "cognitive stimulation" activities.

If the school does not seem suited to your child, shop around. There are many other factors, such as cost and distance from home, which may also affect your decision.

Three year olds have some separation anxieties, so initially accompany your child into the school and remain with her as long as your intuition tells you it is necessary. Be sensitive to your child's anxiety, yet be sure you are not projecting your anxiety onto your child. If mother is anxious, the child will feel it and believe there is something to worry about.

Day care centers versus preschool? *Your* primary need may be day care, particularly if you work outside the home, but at this stage your child needs more than just baby-sitting. Preschools, which are designed to stimulate and educate, naturally provide "day care." You get much more for your money (and so does your child) by enrolling your child in a good preschool rather than depositing him in a day-care center.

Sometimes, whether or not he is ready for a preschool is a question that can only be answered by your child. If you sense a mismatch between your child and either teacher or school, make a change. You want the child's first school to be a positive experience. Concerning placement in a school or any social group, operate on parental intuition: when in doubt, take him out. ■

In this section I will use the term *starting school* to mean "starting school outside the home." Parents who have followed the continuum concept of Christian parenting really started their child's education at his or her birth.

There are two opposing schools of thought about when children should start school. The first believes no child is too young for school. Japanese schools and writers have popularized the advantages of early childhood education. They base their philosophy on the fact that the most rapid development of a child's brain occurs in the first three years. Therefore, this is the period in which a child has the greatest capacity for learning. For example, a young child can easily become bilingual simply by being exposed to two languages simultaneously from early infancy.

Teachers who evaluate these early educational programs vary greatly in the conclusions they draw. Some teachers say children do not necessarily show a higher academic achievement if they begin their formal education early. Some teachers, especially music teachers, report that children pushed into learning before their time often exhibit burnout by the age of eight or ten when most children are beginning to learn music.

One of the best-known advocates of early childhood education was Dr. Maria Montessori, who pointed out that a growing child has "sensitive periods" or stages in which his or her developing brain is most receptive to certain types of learning. I am a strong advocate of the Montessori philosophy of teaching because it is geared to a child-considered environment. A child educated by this method is encouraged to succeed at his or her own rate—*not in comparison with other children.* Work and play are synonymous; a child *learns how to learn* and learning becomes a joy to the child's absorbent mind (a complete description of the advantages of the Montessori method is given in my first book, *Creative Parenting*). It is important to point out that Dr. Montessori developed her philosophy of education for underprivileged children who were neglected in their homes. There is nothing in the Montessori philosophy or method of education that cannot be done just as well by a caring parent in a child-considered environment at home. (See the Bibliography for suggested readings on early childhood education.)

An opposing school of thought to these "early starters proponents" is the growing home school movement, which advocates teaching your child at home until he is about ten years of age. This movement was popularized by Dr. Raymond Moore in his book *School Can Wait*. The movement to bring education back into the home arose from the same concerns that brought birthing back into the home and babies back on to their mother's breasts. These movements are a tip of the iceberg of a new breed of parents, especially mothers who are no longer content to allow strangers to tell them how to birth, feed, and educate their children. The main reason I am sympathetic with this tendency to bring education back into the home is parents are beginning to place a higher priority on a child's character traits and Christian values than on early reading, writing, and arithmetic.

Another reason for the growing popularity of home schools is the concept of peer dependency. I have mentioned that by middle childhood your child begins either to accept or reject your values. How many of the values he accepts or rejects depends on the degree of competition your child receives from alternative value systems. Parents who would like to teach their children at home have made the decision that the options of education in their community are unacceptable because the schools' value systems compete with that of the home. These parents also have the real concern that the child's self-esteem actually may be lowered by attending school outside the home, rather than increased. Parents who are considering delaying school entry usually have two major concerns: (1) "Will my child be socially deprived?" and (2) "Will he be academically behind?" Dr. Moore claims that his studies show children who are taught at home tend to become social leaders when they are eventually placed into school systems at the age of ten. They also tend to be academically ahead of those children taught in the usual school system, which is probably due to the fact that they receive much more one-on-one teaching than children in the average over-crowded classroom.

The age at which you send your child to school and whether or not you educate him at home depend upon *your total family situation*. What is important is that you base your decision upon whether school will be an extension of your family's Christian values and will contribute positively to your child's self-esteem. You do have choices in education just as you had choices in childbirth. Consider what is best for your individual child in your individual family situation regardless of what are the norms of the neighborhood. If, after much prayer and counsel, you have decided to teach your child at home and delay school entry, expect to get some flack from your friends and/or family. If you decide to set up your own home school, suggestions for various activities and curricula are offered in the books listed in the Bibliography under the section on education.

There is an excellent book titled *Summer Children: Ready or Not for School* (see Bibliography) that explores the reasons why every child under the age of five years, six months should wait a year before starting kindergarten. The authors, one of whom has a doctorate in education, another a school psychologist, have done their own research and have reviewed extensive data from other researchers. They feel that what is now expected in kindergarten is simply too much, too soon, for too many, often resulting in learning disabilities as the child progresses through school.

If you decide to enroll your child in a kindergarten or first grade at the traditional age of five or six, your next decision is whether or not to send your child to a Christian school. Parents, I strongly encourage you to do so if the logistics of your community and your finances permit. Sending him or her to a Christian school can give your child a head start toward a Christ-centered life. However, you should be just as selective in choosing a Christian school as you were in choosing a pediatrician. While a Christian school is no guarantee that your child will be surrounded only with committed Christians, it simply lowers the risk that your child will be exposed to persons of significance who will compete with your Christian values.

I object to the philosophy of exposing a young child to a public school because it prepares him more for the real world. For what or for whom are you ultimately preparing your child, for the world or for Christ? Exposing your child to all of the options so that he can choose his own path is not only scripturally unsound (Prov. 22:6), but in most cases, a child left to himself will not choose the path to Christ without some direction from persons of significance around him. Even in a Christian school your child will be exposed to varying levels of commitment to Christ. There will be deeply committed Christian children from deeply committed Christian homes who will minister to your child, and there also will be children from lukewarm Christian or non-Christian homes to whom your child can minister. For example, one day a nine year old attending a Christian school confided in me, "My mom and dad sent me to a Christian school hoping that some of the Christian teachings will rub off on me and just help to keep me out of trouble, but they really don't believe in Christ."

Another reason I object to public schools is the exposure your child will get to the religion of secular humanism and New Age philosophy. An excellent book on this subject is written by Johanna Michaelsen, *Like Lambs to the Slaughter* (Eugene, OR: Harvest House, 1989).

How to Get the Most Out of Your Child's School

Choosing your child's school is only the beginning; you need to keep your finger on the pulse of the classroom. Don't leave all of your child's Christian teaching to his or her teachers. I strongly maintain that a child's primary Christian education must come from the home and must be complemented by the school and the church. Visit the classroom frequently. Become deeply acquainted with your child's teachers to the extent that you honestly know what their values are. The school is only as good as the parents behind it, and the standards of any school are only as high as the parents demand.

Show your child's teachers you value their profession and regard them as an extension of your home. A suggestion that will help you convey this is to invite each teacher at least once a year to your home for dinner and an evening discussion of how you value your child's education. Pray for your child's teachers asking God to give them the wisdom to discipline and nurture your child in the ways of the Lord. Convey to your child's teachers that you are praying for them. One of my greatest joys as a pediatrician is hearing the parents of one of my little patients tell me they are praying for me.

Keep your eyes on the classroom and be involved in the daily activity of the school. The attitude and atmosphere of a Christian school should carry out the admonition of the Lord in Deuteronomy 6:6–9, in which God tells us to saturate the child's environment with instructions about Himself. A Christian school that is living up to its name should encourage an atmosphere of love for one another, making its Christianity self-evident and a model for non-Christian schools.

A Christian school should focus more on how a child feels than how he learns. Unfortunately this is not always the case. In order to justify their existence, perhaps Christian schools have become defensive trying to compete with the public school system. Many Christian schools are so preoccupied with how their children compare academically with children in the public school system that they lose sight of the basic fact that all Christian psychologists teach: A Christian school should be more prepared than a public school to help the child who fails to learn, because he probably has a fragile self-esteem. Unfortunately, most Christian schools are not equipped to meet the needs of special children.

Have a proper attitude about homework. A typical complaint I hear from parents is, "My eight year old refuses to do his homework, and each night it becomes a hassle to get the work done. I am tired of getting on my child's back to complete his assignments." Because this is a common problem, let me offer an opinion about homework for the elementary school child. I believe children below grade six should not have homework or should have no more than twenty minutes of homework a night. I base this opinion upon the observation that homework is a negative experience for most young children. Also, I feel the main objective in sending a child to school in the early elementary school years is to develop a positive attitude toward learning; a secondary objective is to impart information. The homework hassle often creates a poor attitude in the child about school in general, and this may interfere with his total educational experience.

Unless a child has a specific learning problem that requires remedial help at home, both teachers and parents should set up the educational schedule at school so that the child has enough time during the day to complete his assignments. If homework is assigned, it should be in the form of a creative project that the parents and child can do *together*, and it should not just be filling out a workbook or carrying the same routine classroom teaching into the home. Because of the demands of the educational system of children and the demanding work schedules of parents, there is diminishing time at home for spiritual training and for parents and children simply to enjoy each other. This is especially true for parents who work long hours, for single parents, and for parents who send their children to day care after school.

The two most common reasons children give me for not doing their homework are "It's boring" and "I'm tired." These are justifiable complaints. For example, if a child is learning about plants in school, his homework should not be reading and writing about plants (which should be done at school); his "homework" should be his own garden. In the later elementary school years a certain amount of homework discipline may be necessary to prepare the child for the increased demands of high school.

■ Breakfast for a Growing Brain

New research on feeding school-age children has revealed an exciting connection between what children eat and how well they learn. Here are some tips on giving your young student a healthy breakfast.

If your hectic household is like morning rush hour in our home, sleepy kids and hurried parents don't have time for healthy breakfasts. Yet, studies show that children who begin their day with a balanced breakfast show better school performance than those who don't. Breakfast eaters are likely to make higher grades, pay closer attention, participate more in class discussions, and are able to manage more complex academic problems. Breakfast skippers, on the other hand, are more likely to be inattentive, sluggish, and make lower grades. Also, the type of breakfast a child eats can influence learning and behavior. Studies show that school children perform best when they eat a breakfast containing both protein and complex carbohydrates, such as yogurt and granola or eggs and toast. For a sweet touch, add some fresh fruits to these combinations.

Your child's growing brain contains trillions of nerves. At the end of each nerve are tiny feelers that are trying to reach out and connect with other nerves. The better these connections, the better your child learns. Throughout the brain biochemical messengers, called neurotransmitters, help the developing brain make the right connections. Food influences these neurotransmitters, and a meal of proteins and carbohydrates seems to be the most brain-friendly food for thought. Why this food-mood connection? Complex carbohydrates, such as healthy cereals, are like time-release packets of energy that fuel the brain. Adding protein to complex carbohydrates (such as dairy and grain) help the neurotransmitters in the brain work better. Sugars, such as icings and syrups, for breakfast are not friendly to learning, since they cause a roller-coaster effect. The blood sugar skyrockets and then plummets mid- or late-morning, causing the child's attention to waver and behavior to deteriorate. Healthy breakfast foods, like dairy, grains, and fruits, provide a more steady supply of energy for the young student's brain. Of course, it's what you eat, not what you say, that impresses a child. By treating yourself to a healthy breakfast, you model to your children that eating a healthy breakfast gives the whole family a smart nutritional start. ■

How to Give Your Child an Educational Advantage at Home

Home education for the young child practices the principles of Christian continuum parenting. Since parents who practice these parenting styles know their children better, they know intuitively how to educate them. The child who is a product of this level of parenting *feels right*. The child who feels right is more likely to learn right because this child is at peace with himself, and his mind is therefore more receptive to learning. As Hannah waited to wean Samuel from his home to his education at the temple, so must you decide when your child is ready to be weaned from the security of his family to an education outside the home. The concept of home learning I wish parents to appreciate is what I call the "educational continuum." A young child who is exposed at his own comfortable pace to an enriched environment of meaningful activities that enhance his God-given skills *feels more valuable as a person*. The more the absorbent mind of the preschool child is exposed to an environment of learning, the more he wants to learn. The more the outside world becomes interesting to him, the more he becomes interesting to himself and to others. The fulfilled child enjoys learning because he enjoys the good feeling that results from having his curiosity satisfied. Parents who have created a home environment that allows their child's individual talents to flourish at his own individual pace have given the child a real educational advantage. When the child begins more formal schooling outside the home, gaining information will be given priority over attitudes about learning.

What about the child who is the product of a less stimulating environment? If her parents do not stimulate her curiosity and if she has no model to imitate at home, she is without direction. If her curiosity is not satisfied, she becomes less curious. If she is not challenged, she becomes less motivated. An example of an unstimulated child is the child who is parked for many hours each day in front of the television set to be pacified and entertained. This child resigns herself to a lower level of fulfillment. She becomes passive and uninteresting, to herself and to others. A dull and wasted child becomes an unhappy child. The result of this break in the natural educational continuum is that the child's desire to learn operates at a lower level. Because the unfulfilled child has not developed a joy of learning and a positive attitude toward learning in her earlier years, while her interest and curiosity were at their peaks, she is suddenly overwhelmed with information when she enters kindergarten or the first grade. She then may become less interested in learning, may rebel against the system, and is prey to being classified as having a learning disability. The following suggestions will help you stimulate your child's educational environment. (See Bibliography for further reading on this subject.)

1. *Select toys appropriate for your child's age and stage of development.* Choose toys that teach as well as amuse and that demonstrate the cause-and-effect relationship.

2. *Enrich your child's language studies.* Studies have shown that *active language* input (the child is being directly talked with) is one of the prime determinants of personality and educational development.

3. *Read to your child.* Children love to read *with* others. I emphasize *with* because children enjoy books well before they have the ability to read. When you are reading with your child, try to relate the pictures in the book with scenes in real life so that your child's mind does not become confused by too much picture-book fantasy. Books are often the entree to what I call "expansion" learning. Use his books as an opener and expand on certain themes. For example, if your child points to a tree in the book, expand on his interest by taking him outside and showing him a variety of trees. You may even climb up into the tree or watch the birds in it. These short periods of spontaneous learning are often more meaningful than large blocks of planned teaching.

4. *Give your child a large pad of paper, a variety of crayons, and some rulers.* The blank sheet encourages more creativity than coloring predesigned figures. Arts and crafts stimulate a child's fine motor development, creativity, and sense of accomplishment. The young child loves recognition for his or her artistic creations even if it is a simple blob of watercolors on a sheet of paper. For this reason, display your child's primitive artwork around your house, such as on the refrigerator door. This is a real boost for your child's desire to create. She feels that Mommy and Daddy are interested in what she makes; what she makes must be pretty good; therefore, she must be pretty good.

5. *Build things with your child.* Expensive "designer" toys are not necessary for giving your child an enriched environment. Children three years old and younger enjoy building things. A simple set of blocks and canister-like containers in your kitchen are good starter toys. Older children love to build with scrap lumber. I feel every family ought to have a pile of scrap lumber outside the house for a child to build with.

Let me share with you an example of how you can get a lot of mileage out of simple and inexpensive toys. One Christmas when our first two children were five and seven years old we decided to buck the commercial Christmas and not succumb to filling our home with a bunch of plastic toys. I went down to the local lumberyard and filled our station wagon with end cuts of scrap lumber. The night before Christmas I dumped the lumber on the basement floor with a couple of hammers and boxes of assorted nails. Our children still remember that pile of lumber as one of their best Christmas presents. It lasted several years and encouraged creative carpentry (just like Jesus' carpentry!).

6. *Music should play an important role in your child's education.* Infants and children are usually very attentive to good music. Studies show that young children are usually more attentive to classical music, perhaps because the orderly nature of classical music fits in with the developing order in a child's mind. Make music lessons available for your young child and encourage him to develop a musical skill according to his own interest and talent levels. Accomplishing a musical skill contributes greatly toward a child's total fulfillment. Music also provides a form of family entertainment. Some of the happiest families I have seen are families that sing and play music together for both enjoyment and fellowship. Music is also a beautiful vehicle with which the young child can learn to praise God.

7. *Use God's world of nature as one big textbook for your child.* Your backyard, the woods, the beach, the mountains, the sky, the sun, the moon, the stars are all fascinating to a child. Tiny bugs and insects are also interesting because children are fascinated with smallness and minute detail. Plant a little garden with your child so that he can see what God allows to develop from a tiny seed nourished in fertile soil. Not only do gardens fulfill a child's sense of accomplishment and of reward for efforts, but they also provide a natural opportunity for you to discuss God's creation and the origins of life.

8. *Provide opportunities for your child to develop awareness of his or her body.* Gymnastics, sports, and artistic dance such as ballet will help your child develop

and appreciate the body God has designed for him or her.

These suggestions are just a few of the many activities that *fulfill* a child. I have strong feelings that parents should help their child develop his talents and creativity so that he is able to stimulate, satisfy, and amuse himself from *within*. The fulfilled child is able to derive satisfaction and avoid boredom by reading a book, creating an art or craft, playing a musical instrument, devising a game, or engaging in an exchange of humor (humor plays a very important part in the educational development of a child). One of the reasons parents should strive to help their child be fulfilled from within is that today's child is surrounded by a world of instant turnons and gratification from the use of material things. Many children become preoccupied with passively entertaining themselves and feel they need to be constantly amused or they will get bored. A child who needs to be entertained passively or who needs a material gadget for fulfillment is susceptible to being unfulfilled as an adult.

What About the Child Who Fails to Learn?

The term *learning disability* is a relative term. The American educational system grades children on a bell-shaped curve, and most children in the middle of this curve can function adequately within the system. However, children at either end of this curve may have great difficulty learning within the system *as compared* to the other children. The current system of school entry and grade progression is based upon a child's age rather than his mental maturity. About 10 percent of grade school children experience varying degrees of difficulty learning all the subjects according to the methods used in the present system. Children who learn within the present system have "learning abilities"; those who do not learn within the present system are labeled as having "learning disabilities." Not only does a child with this label not measure up to the expectations of the educational system into which he or she has been placed but, what is more important, the child does not learn *as compared to the other children*. Continued exposure of a fragile child to comparison gradually leads to diseases of low self-esteem. A child with a disability in academic performances may eventually have an even greater "disability" in his or her self-esteem. Because a child's academic performance and his self-esteem are so intimately related, it is often difficult to determine whether how a child learns is a result of how he feels or whether how he feels is a result of how he learns.

Intuitive parents and teachers can and should be alert to a child's maladjustment to school. If you have met your child's teachers and have kept abreast of her classroom situation, you are likely to foresee her reaction to this new environment. Knowing your child's teachers, or parent substitutes, enables them to know your child better.

The high-need child is indeed a candidate for developing school problems. Just as the high-need child needs above-average parenting, he also needs above-average schooling. Parents who have trained this high-need child according to principles of Christian attachment parenting have developed a wider acceptance of his behavior. Some of these high-need children do not indicate their temperaments until they enter school, primarily because a school has a narrower range of acceptance than the home and a child is made to conform to a system that does not know him. Also, the high-need child receives more one-to-one input from his parents at home.

If you have identified your child as a high-need child, select a school that is sensitive to his individual needs. The mismatch between child and school is one of the most common causes of learning disabilities. This mismatch should be called a "teaching disability" rather than a "learning disability." Many children designated as having learning disabilities are actually brilliant children who learn quickly and become bored by the classroom situation. Because they are labeled "dumb," they feel dumb and eventually act dumb. Children are very quick to feel and act according to the labels they perceive the persons of significance around them have given them.

There are specific signs of impending school problems. Boredom is usually the earliest sign. A child becomes bored with himself and bored with his performance at school. Another sign is diminishing enthusiasm. While it is unrealistic to expect a child to jump out of bed and rush off to school without an occasional grumble, most of the time your child has some spark of enthusiasm about going to school. Most children have an inborn desire to learn. If presented properly, learning should be enjoyed by most children most of the time.

Watch for the slow adjuster. Most children are very resilient and adaptable to the transition from home to school or from one grade to another. However, some children do not adjust to change easily and need a higher level of sensitivity during these transitional periods. This is why most behavioral problems appear at the transition from one developmental or educational stage to another. The high-need child often has trouble being compliant.

School phobias are another sign of impending school problems. If your child presents an increasing number of vague physical complaints that occur with regularity the night or morning before school and sub- side on weekends and holidays, suspect that a fear of leaving home or attending school or both may be the underlying causes of these physical complaints.

Behavioral problems are often related to poor school performance. Children are generally very vulner- able to any attacks on their self-esteem and protect themselves at all costs. A child who does not receive strokes from academic performance usually will seek alternative methods of recognition in school, such as being the class clown. Undesirable behavior in the class- room often carries over into undesirable behavior at home.

A step-by-step approach to helping your child who fails to learn is discussed in detail in my book *Creative Parenting*. I cannot overemphasize the importance of getting at the root of poor school performance. I would have to rate the diagnosis of school problems as the most mismanaged problem of childhood. In my experi- ence, most school problems ultimately are traced back to diseases of self-esteem. Some children do indeed have specific learning disabilities that prevent them from learning in the way most children are able to learn; however, today's school system is more ready to diag- nose and treat these problems.

Exercise much prayer and consultation to get at the source of your child's learning problem. Your main "treatment" is to focus more on how she feels rather than on how she learns. Rather than devoting your attention to activities that relate directly to your child's learning, concentrate on having *fun* with your child. Direct most of your energy toward activities that contribute to her general self-esteem with the view that any improvement in her sense of well-being is likely to carry over in her ability to learn.

Part 4

Special Topics in Parenting

CHAPTER 9

SEXUALITY EDUCATION IN ADOLESCENCE

Most children in the middle childhood and adolescent ages are just as uncomfortable being approached with sexuality education as their parents are uncomfortable approaching them. For this reason, it is important to create the proper setting for sexuality education. Don't suddenly pick a night and get it over with by announcing, "Tonight we are going to talk about sex." Children are very mood dependent when it comes to most forms of learning, especially learning about sex. When your child gives you a cue that he is interested and receptive to some meaningful parent-child dialogue about the topic, plan a special outing that allows you and your child to communicate freely. If you already have created a series of these special times together, your child may give you a few openers of his own.

The period of middle childhood is often described as a time of "normal homosexuality." Boys tend to stick with boys and girls stick with girls, and gender lines are seldom crossed between the ages of eight and ten.

Comparing genitals between members of the same sex is common at this age, especially among boys: "I'll show you mine if you show me yours." This period is also called a "latent" or "dormant" period because in many children there seems to be a decrease in the rate of growth and in sexual interest. While this may be a latent period for your child, it should not be a latent period for you. This is an important time for providing correct sexual information and for forming sexual attitudes for adolescent sexuality. This is the age when you are competing with the sex education your child gets outside the home. Being comfortable with and interested in presenting proper sexuality education to your child at this age avoids the "blind leading the blind" approach of street-corner sex education. Children often become very private about their bodies at this age and become increasingly uncomfortable with parental nudity. When you sense these feelings of modesty, develop discretion about your personal nudity.

Sexuality Education in School

Sex education in school is a controversy that faces most parents when their children are about ten years old. Parents certainly have a right to know who is teaching their children what and when, and the school needs to be sensitive to the parents' feelings. I always have maintained that a school is only as good as the parents behind it. The main problem with sex education is that it is impossible to separate sexual facts from sexual values. Even in Christian schools, the value systems of parents vary greatly; therefore, it is hard to agree on a curriculum of sex education in a particular school. Opponents of sex education in schools feel that information fosters interest and encourages more sexual activity. They also legitimately fear that their own values will be undermined. Advocates of sex education in schools suggest that at least adolescents be given a better understanding of sexuality in order to make more responsible decisions about their own sexual behavior.

The real facts are that today's adolescents are more sexually active than previous generations were, but their sexuality education is no better. However, I am uncomfortable with the attitude that the responsibility to correct this deficiency belongs to the school. Unfortunately, like so many other government programs, the school must assume responsibility because many parents are not doing their job at home. Ideally, the information and attitudes of sexuality education should be taught and lived at home. The school should be an extension of this home education by providing a dimension the home cannot provide, such as group discussion. Group discussion about adolescent sexuality is the main benefit of sexuality education in the schools. Perhaps this discussion on sexuality education would be presented better at your church than at your school. Since a developed and agreed upon set of sexual values is often the number one controversy, parents are more likely to agree upon a set curriculum and values within their church than within a school, which usually has a wider range of value systems.

The following suggestions can help the home, the church, and the school work together to impart not only accurate sexual information but, more importantly, Christian attitudes about sexuality.

Keep your eye on the classroom. Be involved in selecting the curriculum and be sure you know the basic values of the person or persons who will be teaching the class. It is amazing that absolutely damaging instruction can get into our school systems. I remember reviewing a proposed curriculum for sex education for a high school. In the section on birth control, abortion was presented as an accepted norm and abstinence was presented way down on the list of birth control. Parents ought to examine thoroughly all parts of the curriculum down to every chapter and verse. If a course doesn't meet your moral standards, you can refuse to allow your child to attend.

Sexuality education should be presented as part of a general biology course, such as "how the body works," and should not be marketed as a sex education course.

Sexuality education never should be lumped with discussions of alcohol and drug abuse. Sexuality is a normal, healthy part of Christian living; drugs and alcohol are not.

Group discussions should be encouraged. General topics focusing mostly on the anatomy and physiology of the reproductive organs may be taught with boys and girls together in a class, and with group discussions encouraged. More personal elements of sex education such as menstruation, hygiene, and wet dreams are taught more comfortably in separate classes of boys and girls.

Schools need to reject the message that everybody is sexually active. Just at the age when an adolescent is attempting to formulate his own values and make decisions, some sex education courses send him mixed messages: premarital sex is not advised but everybody is doing it. This may indeed be true in many schools, but in many schools and homes traditional Christian values are still adhered to and everybody is *not* doing it.

Schools should make a special effort to present premarital abstinence as the norm.

Parents, pray and be vigilant, keeping your finger on the pulse of the classroom. If you blindly turn your child over to peer dependency and the value system that prevails in his or her school, you run the risk of creating an adolescent with a low sexual self-esteem. Sexuality education should encourage the development of a sexually informed and sexually responsible adolescent whose emotions are under the control of his or her God-fearing Christian values. If your child is in a public school that violates your values, take an active part in changing the sex education course. (See Bibliography for suggested reading on this subject.)

Dating

"When should I allow my teenager to date?" is another common question from parents. Because dating readiness varies among teenagers, I will offer some general suggestions that will help you decide when your teenager should be allowed to date. It is tempting to follow the crowd to avoid being called old-fashioned, but, parents, cling to your Christian beliefs; the crowd is not going in the right direction. I would suggest you not be old-fashioned if the "new fashion" were working, but it isn't.

Teenagers are more sexually assertive and active than ever before. Diseases of sexual irresponsibility are rampant: teen pregnancy, venereal disease, and divorce. Men and women are remaining single longer than ever before. In many cultures, men and women date late and marry early; in this culture they date early and marry late. I feel God did not design males and females to be in close contact in the single state for so long. Since today's educational and economic systems encourage marrying later, it stands to reason that there should be some modification of the present unrestricted dating practices, certainly in Christian homes. Parents, in today's sexual climate, without God's help, it is totally unrealistic to expect teenagers who are going steady to adhere to sexual abstinence. God did promise He would not let people be tempted beyond what they can handle and that he would provide a way out in order that they can stand up under temptation (1 Cor. 10:13). He also said to "flee sexual immorality" (1 Cor. 6:18). It is on these foregoing considerations that I base the following suggestions for Christian dating practices.

What Is a Date?

To many parents, the term *date* is one of those four-letter words that remind them of the social and sexual maturity of their adolescents. It implies some sort of contract, an agreement between two members of the opposite sex to be together for a certain occasion. There is a certain "I'm yours" commitment to the term *date*. In Christian teaching, dating is considered a preparatory stage for mate selection. The young teenager may not have such a sophisticated view of dating.

Mixed-group activities, particularly church group activities, should be encouraged for children before their teenage years. Properly chaperoned mixed parties encourage boys and girls to enjoy one another as individuals before the attraction between the sexes is physical. These mixed-group activities encourage children to learn how to relate to both sexes in the "comfort in numbers" setting.

The next stage of boy-girl activities is *group dating,*

in which boys and girls in their early teens attend properly chaperoned activities as couples. This is the initial form of dating. Depending on the individual circumstances, group dating should be a healthy stage of sexual maturity for the young adolescent. Group dating brings the adolescent out of himself or herself and should have a maturing effect on the otherwise egocentric teenager. This may be the first time the adolescent acknowledges any other person to be as important as himself. The next stage of dating is *single dating*, which today usually means a boy and a girl and a car. This is a level of dating that is of most concern to parents. The following discussion pertains to single dating.

When Should My Teenager Be Allowed to Date?

The age of dating readiness is as variable as the age of puberty. The desire to date usually parallels the puberty level of the adolescent and his or her temperament. One of our boys showed interest in dating at thirteen, another at seventeen. The next variable is the responsibility level of the teenager. Some are more responsible at an earlier age than others. Impulse control is another variable.

A teenager who has proven he is able to control his impulses in nonsexual matters is more likely to be able to control his impulses in sexual matters. What is the level of Christian conscience development in your teenager? Dating is a higher step on the privilege-responsibility ratio. These are the reasons dating readiness cannot be defined absolutely by age alone.

Parents, do not be reluctant to assert your authority on permission to date. This is one of the final steps in the long continuum of discipline and is another example of where your God-given authority is on the line. Teenagers intuitively expect parents to act as their authority and wisdom in giving permission to date. The following is a common scenario. Mary is a freshman in high school. Tom, a senior, invites her out on a single date. Mary does not feel ready but feels peer pressure to begin dating. Mary consults her dad, who says no. Mary then says to Tom, "Sorry, my dad won't let me date yet." Dad is the scapegoat, and Mary is off the hook. Mary later confides in her dad, "Thanks, Dad, I really didn't want to go anyway." Like so many stages in childhood discipline, the child (in this case, the teenager) expects the parent to assume the authority in circumstances when he cannot say no himself.

Parents, don't be too quick to allow your teenager to fling himself or herself into the habit of constant dating in which all of the adolescent's time is spent with members of the opposite sex. Healthy dating should have a positive effect on the adolescent's self-esteem. However, in the most healthy dating progression of sexuality development, it is vitally important for an adolescent to be comfortable relating to members of the *same* sex in order to develop a healthy relationship with the opposite sex.

What About Going Steady?

This level of dating is the accepted dating style in most high schools. Going steady is a real boost for a teenager's self-esteem. Most of these going-steady infatuations are short-lived and many teenagers will go steady many times during their high school and college years.

If at all possible, encourage your teenager to date around. Many teenagers go steady because they are more interested in the security of a relationship than they are interested in their dates as people. This level of commitment deprives a teenager of the ability to mature his or her own personality by learning to relate to many members of the opposite sex. It is also unrealistic to expect a teenage boy and girl who are constantly together to continue sexual abstinence very long.

There is a healthy progression in a relationship between the two sexes: (1) the personal level, (2) the affectionate level, and (3) the physical level. It is important for an adolescent to experience a variety of personal and affectionate levels, but going steady encourages his dating relationship to be spent at the physical level. If you sense that a steady dating relationship is developing for your teenager, discuss it with him in a dialogue that is caring and wise.

What About Predating Counseling?

Discussing dating with your teenager follows the same formula as administering any other disciplinary action with your child; you may not agree with each other but you need to understand where each other is coming from. Approach your teenager with love, and use Scripture as the basis for your discussion. To make a case for sexual purity, cite 1 Corinthians 6:12–13, Ephesians 6:13, and Romans 8:9. Your teenager may not protect himself with the values he grew up with, but it is important he feels you will remain his friend in the face of disappointment.

What About Dating a Non-Christian?

The Bible takes a clear stand on the issue of relationships with non-Christians: "Do not be unequally yoked together with unbelievers. . . . What part has a believer with an unbeliever?" (2 Cor. 6:14–15).

Christian dating practices should contribute to the spiritual growth of both parties. I advise parents not to allow their teenager to date anyone who is not growing as a Christian. The concept of "missionary dating" (dating to bring someone to Christ) is a potentially dangerous practice and parents ought to discourage it. Most teenagers are still growing as Christians themselves and do not have the spiritual control to overcome their sexual impulses. Dating another Christian is certainly no guarantee of sexual purity, but it does add one more important restriction to the teenager's new sexuality. Since dating is a prelude to marriage and since marriage to a nonbeliever is an extremely foolish and risky proposition, eliminate this possibility by urging your teenager to date only Christians.

Christian parents should impress upon their dating teenagers the responsibility they have for influencing the sexual maturity of their dates. The teenage boy has the responsibility for influencing how the teenage girl views men in general, and the teenage girl influences how the teenage boy perceives women.

Teenage Sexuality

Teen pregnancy is one of today's most common medical problems, and it is currently reaching epidemic proportions, even among Christian teenagers. In the past few years in the United States, at least one million teenage girls have become pregnant each year.

Teenagers are sexually active and become pregnant for many reasons. Some teenagers do not fully understand their sexuality and deny that they are candidates for pregnancy. Their sexuality education often has been inadequate and their precautions ineffective. Sexually active teenagers do not use contraceptives reliably. They may feel that contraceptives delete the spontaneity of sex, or are conscience-pricking reminders that they are sexually active—or they simply forget to use them. In my experience, one common characteristic underlies many teen pregnancies—a poor self-image. The teenage girl who has a poor self-image may feel pregnancy proves her femininity and fulfills a need. A teenager may also form a sexual alliance to fill a void in his or her life because of lack of success or identification at home or at school. A teenager girl may become sexually active following a family divorce or the death of her father, or if she has a chronic medical illness, she may use pregnancy as proof of her health.

Attachment parenting can bolster your teen's self-image and can reinforce the values he has learned in your home, thereby minimizing the risk of teen pregnancy, but other preventive measures are available to you. Involve your teenager in extracurricular activities. A teenager who is involved in school activities, sports, and church activities is less likely to seek sexual activities as a means of gratification. Also, be aware of the message your teenager receives from the secular world. For example, the health department provides booklets from Planned Parenthood entitled *Eight Popular Ways for Having Intercourse . . . That Most Smart Teenagers Would Use*, *The Perils of Puberty*, and *So You Don't Want to Be a Sex Object*. A proper sexuality education is the best way to prevent your teenager's being influenced by organizations such as Planned Parenthood.

Another "parental contraceptive" is to insist on Christian dating practices. The sexual urges of teenagers have not changed throughout the past generations. They have always had these urges which were designed by God. What has changed is that today's teenagers are surrounded by many models and persons of significance who encourage them to become sexually active. Because the competition for children's values is increasing, your responsibility to teach them Christian values must also increase. If they do not get these values at home, they are vulnerable to the shallow values of the secular world. Get your child used to a *higher standard of loving* inside his home so he will expect the same away from home. However, dating a Christian is certainly no guarantee that your young person will not be tempted or even pressured to be sexually active. It is important that you convey the importance of chastity in the life plan God has for your child. In our family we discuss this openly and use teachable moments to reinforce our values, having a feel for the pulse of our teen's social life. A good book we have used with our older teens is Josh McDowell's *Why Wait?* (see Bibliography).

Contraceptives

Whether or not to prescribe contraceptives for a sexually active teenager is a difficult dilemma for a physician. Prescribing contraceptives implies he or she is condoning a sinful act. On the other hand, an unprotected sexually active teenager mostly likely will become pregnant. There is only one prescription available to the Christian physician: I believe Christian doctors should share the duty of counseling teenagers to exercise sexual purity.

Pregnancy

Premarital pregnancy should bring out the best in Christian love between parents and their child. If you are presented with this family crisis, convey to your son or daughter, "We care and we are going to help." You can accept your teenager as a person who is in trouble and needs help without condoning his or her actions. Your teen probably feels guilty enough and is embarrassed to talk to you. A concerned third party, such as your pastor or your physician, can bring you together in this time of need.

Your teenager is now faced with several difficult decisions. As a Christian doctor, I advise teenagers to carry their babies to term and insist that they have adequate medical care during their pregnancies. Teenagers who receive good prenatal care are no more susceptible to medical problems during pregnancy than any other age group, but the danger of teenage pregnancy has been popularized because most teenagers do not have proper prenatal care and are more likely to suffer obstetrical complications.

The teenage couple who carry a baby to term must decide whether to raise the baby or give it up for adoption. Although this decision is very difficult, *it is their decision to make alone*. The great majority of forced teenage marriages end in divorce; there is a high incidence of child abuse among the children of teenage parents; teen parents usually deprive themselves of further education and are relegated to the status of welfare roles. My heart goes out to the pregnant teenage girl who, following much prayer and consultation, decides to raise her baby alone. I feel the church should extend the same Christian caring to this mother and child that they extend to widows and orphans.

Abortion

The third option that is often presented to a pregnant teenager is that of abortion. This option is not open to a Christian teenager. Because abortion is commonly presented by the humanistic social planners, I feel it is necessary to go into some detail in presenting the Christian attitude toward abortion. Because of the impact of current abortion laws on today's youth, I have chosen to face this problem head-on as a concerned Christian physician and parent rather than evade the subject because it is too "touchy" to be presented in a baby book. Abortion is not a religious issue, it is a human issue that has far-reaching implications on the physical and moral development of today's youth. Whether your personal opinion is pro-life or pro-abortion, consider the following Christian principles in deciding that abortion should not be available to the pregnant teenager.

The basic concerns I have about abortion are *the act* and *the attitude* of abortion. The act of deliberately aborting a fetus, no matter how you rationalize it, is the act of taking a human life. Since taking a human life is wrong, the obvious solution to this dilemma is to define the fetus as "not a human life," and this is exactly what the Supreme Court has done. In 1973, the Supreme Court proclaimed that "the fetus is not a person; legal personhood does not exist prenatally" (*Roe v. Wade,* January 23, 1973). When many states disagreed with the federal decision, the states' opinions were termed *unconstitutional* by the federal government. In no other moral blunder has a decision of so few affected the lives of so many. In this historical decision, the federal government not only usurped individual states' rights, but it also deprived a segment of this population unable to defend themselves of the right to life.

To understand how ridiculous this court decision

was, consider what this "nonperson" can do. As early as one month after conception, this nonperson has a beating heart; by a month and a half, brain waves can be measured on his developing brain; by two months, he can grasp an object placed in his hand; by three months he has a functioning brain, can urinate, defecate, sleep, see, hear, and feel pain. All of his limbs and organs are formed by three months, and they mature throughout the remainder of the pregnancy. Only because immaturity forces him to derive food and oxygen from his mother does he give up his right to personhood because a court has so ruled. It is interesting that the absence of brain waves and a heartbeat is accepted as medical death but the presence of a heartbeat and brain waves are not accepted as "medical life."

When the abortion-on-demand laws were liberalized, the fetus could be killed legally *at any time before term*. Occasionally an aborted baby is born alive "by mistake," and nothing is more embarrassing to the abortionist than delivering a live baby. In a few court trials where a baby has been killed after delivery, the abortionist was legally acquitted on the grounds that the baby was "intended to be an abortion." Just how far can the law be stretched, and where will it end?

These abortion-on-demand laws give the mother and society the right to kill a baby because the baby is either inconvenient for the mother or unsuitable for society. The advocates of abortion claim that abortion is an issue of women's rights and that women should have complete control over their bodies. If the fetus were like an inflamed appendix whose continued presence in the body would jeopardize the health of the mother, then it should be removed. The fetus has committed no crime. Therefore, should the fetus forfeit his or her right to life?

Abortion is marketed as the answer to the teen pregnancy problem and the medical profession has been lured into this mess by feeling obligated to provide a "service" to meet the growing demand. Since the rise in the pregnancy rate among teenagers parallels the easy availability of abortions, could it be that the abortion-on-demand laws are actually contributing to teen pregnancy and encouraging teenagers to be less sexually responsible? It is unfortunate that even members of the medical profession have allowed themselves to be followers instead of leaders on this issue. When I graduated from medical school, I remember taking the Hippocratic oath: "I will not give to a woman an instrument to produce abortion." I feel that the Supreme Court's decision approving abortions on demand in 1973 was one of the most disastrous moral turning points of this century. Since 1973, more than twenty-seven million unborn children have been destroyed by abortion. Not only is the number of abortions performed annually increasing, but they are also being performed on older and older fetuses. An example of this was the grizzly discovery in California of seventeen thousand aborted babies in a garbage container. A coroner's autopsy determined some of the babies weighed as much as four to five pounds.

The attitude of abortion has even more far-reaching effects on our youth than the act itself. At the very age when teenagers are attempting to grow into responsible people, they learn that they can amend one irresponsible act with another irresponsible act: "I'll simply get an abortion." Pro-abortion propaganda has programmed the vulnerable minds of our youth to rationalize that it is not really a person that is being scraped out and flushed. The subtle moral message is, "Don't think about what *it* is, think about how you are going to get rid of it." The abortion-on-demand laws are the first inch in the yardstick of a complete disregard for the God-given dignity of human life. Feticide (killing the unborn), which is what we really should call abortion, is listed in the public high school sex education programs along with the pill and the IUD as an accepted form of birth control. Since feticide has been marketed as an accepted form of controlling birth, the next logical step is to regard infanticide as an acceptable form of controlling life. An example of this is the case of Infant Doe, a Down's syndrome newborn who was born with a closed esophagus so that food was not able to reach his stomach. If given proper intravenous nourishment, this baby could easily have survived until an operation was performed to correct the deformity of his esophagus. Despite offers made to adopt Infant Doe, the courts upheld the parents' decision to withhold any medical treatment. The baby was allowed to die after seven days of thirst and starvation. Infant Doe's tragic death, and the recent support for partial birth abortions, convinces me that our world is moving toward the philosophy that only those persons who have the health and ability to speak out are those who have the right to life.

The abortion-on-demand laws also convey the attitude to developing youth that there are no absolute laws of right or wrong. The concept of rightness or wrongness is relative to what is convenient to a particular person's circumstances at a given time. Abortion is a classic example of this moral confusion: if a fetus is killed by an assailant, this is called "murder"; if a fetus is killed by an abortionist, this is called "choice."

What Does the Bible Say About Abortion?

One of the most beautiful Scriptures that attest to the personhood of the fetus is Psalm 139:13–16:

> *For You formed my inward parts;*
> *You have covered me in my mother's womb.*
> *I will praise You, for I am fearfully and wonderfully*
> *   made;*
> *Marvelous are Your works,*
> *And that my soul knows very well.*
> *My frame was not hidden from You,*
> *When I was made in secret,*
> *And skillfully wrought in the lowest parts of the earth.*
> *Your eyes saw my substance, being yet unformed.*
> *And in Your book they all were written,*
> *The days fashioned for me,*
> *When as yet there were none of them.*

God's involvement in fetal development is again stated in Jeremiah 1:5: "Before I formed you in the womb I knew you; / Before you were born I sanctified you; / I ordained you a prophet to the nations." Exodus 21:22–25 states that even the "life for a life" penalty could be imposed upon someone who struggled with a woman causing damage or loss of life to her fetus. Genesis 2:7 gives further support to the God-given personhood of the fetus: "And the Lord God formed man of the dust of the ground, and breathed into his nostrils the breath of life; and man became a living being." This passage indicates that it is God's breath of life, the soul, that gives personhood to a living being. Luke 1:44 says that Elizabeth's unborn child leaped for joy at Mary's greeting, suggesting that fetuses feel emotion. Perhaps the most compelling passage supporting the sanctity of human life is in Exodus 20:13: "You shall not murder."

Complications of Abortion

Not only is abortion against God's law, but the high incidence of medical complications following abortions also suggests that abortion is against the natural law of the woman's body. Women who have abortions are more likely to experience sterility, premature births, miscarriages, obstetrical complications, and severe psychiatric breakdowns in subsequent pregnancies. Even with preabortion counseling, guilt may reappear years later when a woman reassesses her past life. All of these complications have far-reaching implications for parents of pregnant teenagers who should be aware that teenagers are able to obtain abortions *without their parents' consent.*

CHAPTER 10

CONTROLLING ELECTRONIC INFLUENCES ON YOUR CHILD

Television

The average child will have watched fifteen thousand hours of television by the time he is eighteen years old. During this time, he will have witnessed eighteen thousand murders and three hundred fifty thousand commercials. Children do not distinguish between learning and entertainment; they learn from everything they see. Most children tend to accept much of what they see on television as being realistic; they are not yet able to distinguish fantasy from reality easily. Therefore, children are likely to learn and remember new forms of aggressive behavior by watching the kind of violence presented in the mass media. By repeated exposure to violence and aggressive behavior, their emotional sensitivity is gradually lessened. A direct relationship exists between the amount of violence a child watches on television and the aggressive behavior he demonstrates. Violent television programs do not relax children or leave them with a good feeling. They create anxiety.

Children also learn unchristian attitudes toward sexuality from TV. Most of the love relationships portrayed on TV are mutually exploitive rather than mutually fulfilling as Christian marriages should be.

Watching television is a passive event. At the stage when you are attempting to teach your child inner fulfillment and impulse control, he learns he can simply push a button and achieve instant gratification without using either his mind or his body. Watching television also fosters a short attention span and poor physical and mental health. More than half the commercials on television advertise foods of questionable nutritional value that are highly sugared and artificially colored and that have detrimental effects on a child's health and behavior. Children younger than eight do not distinguish between program content and commercial content. For example, they may feel that the hero with whom they identify also endorses the products in the commercials.

By watching television, children are made to believe that what they drive, drink, smoke, and wear is what really counts. They hear these messages at the time when they are looking for ways to build up their self-esteem. Children younger than ten actually believe most commercials. And advertisers are masters at producing catchy slogans which may remain in a child's mind for a long time. For example, it is common to hear a three year old singing a television jingle over and over again.

Television presents a world of bright and beautiful people of athletic excellence and of wealth and power, attributes that the child is quick to perceive as respected most by the world. The child who does not see herself as having any of these important characteristics may lose herself in the world of fantasy and imagine herself like her heroes on television. But down deep she may feel she never can be like them. Since building self-esteem is one of our prime goals as parents, TV becomes a competitive teacher.

A Christian Parent's TV Guide

In my family we have wrestled with this electronic prophet of competitive values for a long time. At times we have even considered getting rid of it, which may be unfair and unrealistic. Try the following suggestions to achieve a balanced diet of television watching within your Christian home.

Do not allow indiscriminate TV watching. Convey to your children why indiscriminate TV watching cannot be tolerated within a Christian home. Show them that uncensored television directly opposes God's mandate to parents in Deuteronomy 6:6 and Ephesians 6:4. Convey to them, "I care about what goes into your brain. This is part of my responsibility as your parent for which I will be held accountable by God my Father." You would never allow a stranger to visit or entertain or teach your children without your participation. Why be permissive with television? I have placed this Scripture verse above our TV set: "I will set nothing wicked before my eyes" (Ps. 101:3).

Be selective. Screen the screen. Select which programs your child may or may not watch just as you would approve or disapprove of a book or movie. To help you preselect which programs your child may or may not watch, become involved in organizations that encourage the wise use of television. See the Bibliography for more resource material on discriminate TV watching. There are many entertaining and educational programs on television. Children's horizons can be broadened enormously by this electronic media if it is used correctly and wisely. One particular area of programming parents need to screen more carefully is Saturday morning cartoons. Admittedly this is a time when parents are likely to want the TV to act as a baby-sitter. Sit down and watch the programs your children are being exposed to week after week—you will see sorcery, witchcraft, spell-casting—things all condemned in Scripture (Deut. 18:10–12). Many cartoons are offensively violent. This is a time when a good library of videos can provide the alternative—there is a selection of delightful Bible cartoons, Christian musicals, and adventure stories to choose from.

Watch TV as a family. Neither you nor your children should be allowed to tune into the tube and tune out the rest of your family members. Use commercial time as a time to discuss the messages of the program. If the program or the commercial is contrary to your family values or principles of good health, point out to your children how misleading the message is. This helps them be selective and develop a sense of judgment. No matter how caring and how selective you try to be, occasionally a part of a program may portray unchristian values. Take this opportunity to explain to your children why these values are contrary to the law of God. You may even compare some of the values mentioned on television with specific scriptural passages, again teaching your child that in your house it is the Word of God that will be followed.

Videocassette recorders are a great help in preselecting television programs. A VCR enables you to edit out certain parts of a program that in your opinion compete with the Christian values that prevail in your home.

Alternatives to TV Watching

Having fun as a family does not always mean having some third party entertain you. Family games and activities, such as charades and Bible quizzes, and family projects, such as decorating a room, building a tree house, and planting a garden, are family activities that are much more meaningful than passive TV watching.

Once our TV was broken for six months. During this quiet time, we noticed a marked increase in interpersonal relationships within the family. Our children were playing games and building things together, and we were doing more creative activities together as a family. We read aloud to one another and enjoyed Christian classics. During this experimental period I heard fewer "I'm bored" complaints from our younger children as if they had resigned themselves to a more creative attitude, knowing that the little box was not around to pacify them. I must confess, my own love of sports allowed the tube to be fixed, but later we all agreed we were better off limiting its use. We find our sensitivity heightened when we happen to catch an offensive show. Things that did not bother us before are now offensive to us.

How Much TV Should My Child Watch?

What your child watches on TV is much more important than *how long* he watches TV. I certainly feel the Lord will not bless the home in which children spend more time watching television than they do reading Scripture and praying. If you allow your child to watch one hour of television per day, which I feel should be the maximum, challenge him to read the Word of God for at least half that long or even ten minutes, plus time for prayer. Parents, take charge of the television as part of your mandate to "train a child up in the way he should go."

Other Electronic Influences

Computer and Video Games

The computer probably will have at least as much influence on a child's life as television has since its beginning fifty years ago. It is unrealistic for parents to deny the influences of the personal computer. If the child of tomorrow is going to compete in the world of tomorrow, he probably will have to join the computer age rather than ignore it. Most schools begin training children on computers, and even the Internet, in kindergarten or even earlier if your child attends preschool. Christian parents should be aware of the influences computers can have on their children.

Is the computer becoming a substitute for your child's meaningful interpersonal relationships? Be vigilant to his seeking fulfillment from his computer rather than from God's Word.

Like so many matters in today's materialistic world, the issue of computers, video games, and the Internet is mainly that of balance. As long as children are taught to *use* machines and to *love* people and God, then they have a proper perspective. As they begin to love machines and use people, they are susceptible to drifting farther and farther away from God.

On the subject of video games, in twenty years the number and kinds have mushroomed an incredible amount. PacMan and sports games have been replaced by every type of spectacle imaginable. Many of them are steeped in occultic practices and are no longer subtle in their presentation. Many of the newer games contain graphic violence, some even inviting players to pick up "make believe" weapons and participate in the action. The action and storylines often involve sorcery, witchcraft, or evil spirits. Active participation is encouraged in these things that are condemned in Scripture (Mal. 3:5; Deut. 18:10–12). Be sure you screen video games carefully; take the time to sit down and watch or play with your child so you can teach him or her to discern. And do not let your children go into video arcades unattended, where the images and action cannot be filtered through your eyes.

With the explosion of the Internet in the past few years, parents have a wonderful new learning tool for their children, but they also have a new danger. Chat rooms, sexually explicit websites and other inappropriate sights are now readily accessible to young eyes. There are software programs designed to put access to the Internet in the parents' hands, but parental involvement, instruction, and guidance are still the surest way for your child to get only the best from the computer.

Rock Music

Appreciate the profound effect music has on your child. The average teenager listens to thirty-two hours of music per week, and rock fans are the fastest growing category of music consumers.

Where does rock music fit into the Christian lifestyle? There are two schools of thought on the inherent goodness or evil of rock music. Defenders of rock propose all music is strictly a matter of personal taste; there is nothing inherently unchristian about rock and the lyrics give moral value to a song. Opponents of rock feel the beat of rock music is potentially satanic and erotic. They feel that rock attempts to mesmerize the masses and to provide models of alternative lifestyles to the Christian home.

As a Christian parent, you can arrive at a workable system that respects your God-given responsibility to your child and also respects your child's individual taste for music. Although I have had no in-depth formal education in music appreciation, I feel every individual has a sensitive note that music will touch. If music strikes an individual's note and leaves him feeling right, then that music is right for him. If the music causes disharmony, cacophony, and disorder instead, the music is wrong for that person. The earlier you begin teaching music appreciation to your child, the more finely tuned his or her ear will be.

Your ultimate goal is for your child to make a personal judgment about the intrinsic artistic value of music and to determine whether different kinds of music give him a feeling of rightness within him or an unpleasant feeling of unrightness. Throughout the Bible, especially in the Psalms, worshipers were encouraged to make music to the Lord, and there was a feeling of rightness for having done so. Very early in his childhood, begin playing Christian hymns and classical music for your child in your home. Music lessons during middle childhood add further appreciation for the order of music. By the time he is a teenager, the appreciation of artistic music you will have imparted to your child will be his best defense against the mediocrity that prevails in most of today's rock music.

Listen to the music your teenager enjoys and discuss it with her. It does not suffice to say, "Julie, turn that horrible record off, I can't stand it." This dogmatic and judgmental approach may be unfair and fails to teach your child to be discriminating about the music she selects. Your child probably is thinking, *What's wrong with this music? Is it bad or does Dad simply not like it because it's not his taste?* Take some time out, sit with your child, and listen intently to the record. Write down the lyrics and discuss them. For the great majority of musical pieces, the lyrics give the song its moral value, not the actual beat. Many times teenagers are not even aware of what the lyrics are saying or implying. By taking time to go over the lyrics with your teenager, you are conveying the message to him, "I care about what goes into your mind." This also takes discipline about music out of the realm of personal taste and adds a dimension of credibility to your judgment concerning the basic goodness or badness of a musical composition. Analyzing the lyrics of a song also equips your teenager to be selective and to look beneath its outer shell for some subtle messages that may be unchristian. For example, the entire rock culture is based on a "me first" fulfillment at all costs, using other people and the pleasures of the flesh. Secular rock music allows role models and persons of significance to influence your child's mind and compete directly with the Word of God.

What if your teenager says, "But, Dad, this is a *Christian* rock group"? To most teenagers the term *Christian rock* means only one thing: the lyrics are Christian. It follows, therefore, that if you believe only the lyrics give moral value to a song, then this Christian rock should be accepted into your home.

One of the occupational hazards of parenting a teenager is to be open to his taste in music and not to impose your own upon him unless you have been trained in certain principles of music appreciation. I realized this when I accompanied my teenage son to a Christian rock concert. Although my own musical tastes were offended, I noticed Christian messages were reaching the ears and hearts of teenagers who might not have been reached in any other way.

There are signs that rock music, even Christian rock, is becoming unhealthy for your teenager. One of the most justifiable fears parents have in letting rock music in their home is that their child will model the lifestyle of the composers. Many a teenager's room is papered with record covers and looks like a shrine to these musical idols. The lifestyle of most rock stars bothers parents more than the music. One scriptural reference you may discuss with your child is Luke 6:45: "A good man out of the good treasure of his heart brings forth good; and an evil man out of the evil treasure of his heart brings forth evil. For out of the abundance of the heart his mouth speaks." If you see your child idolizing these rock stars, you have a Christian responsibility to cast these characters out of the house.

Watch for escapism. Because of the widespread marketing of earphones and miniature radios, children literally can escape from the world and blot out all family interruptions or interaction. Too much of this seclusion is not a balanced diet for the developing teenager.

In summary, it is my opinion that rock music of which either the lyrics or the advertised lifestyle of the composers are definitely not Christian should not be allowed in your home. That which relays a Christian message and is sung by Christian people may be allowed into your home. I urge you to guide your teenager in selecting her music as you would guide her in her selection of movies, TV programs, and books.

Movies

The only real way to protect your children from inappropriate movies or videos is to see them yourself first, or ask a trusted, like-minded friend for his opinion. You may want to take the same approach with the music your children listen to: When they bring a movie or tape or CD home, listen to it first, or at least watch the film or listen to the music with them. This way you can discuss the film or music with your children and point out how it measures up to God's Word. You can also have an understanding with your children that you will turn off the movie or music at your discretion.

Families and children are increasingly interested in and aware of movies. The popularity of VCRs has brought the attraction of cinema into our homes. It is necessary to realize that the rating system for movies (G, PG, PG-13, R, and the new NC-17) is not a reliable indicator of a movie's suitability. I have seen one or two R movies that were less offensive than some PG movies. It is usually a mistake to let your children see anything but a G movie without parental guidance. If your children are going to watch a movie at a friend's party, be sure to ask the host or hostess what movie will be shown so you can determine ahead of time how to handle the invitation.

The bottom line in controlling the electronic influences in your child's life is to step in, after prayer and counsel, and call a halt to any influence that in your opinion is competing with your child's walk with Christ.

CHAPTER 11

HELP!
I'M A
SINGLE PARENT

The plight of the single parent is one of the most difficult social problems. Single-parent households are the fastest growing category of all family units. Approximately one out of every two children will spend some part of their childhoods under the care of a single parent. In 1980 in the United States, one million children were being reared by single teenage mothers, and twelve million children under eighteen were living with a single parent.

Although a growing number of women have become single mothers by choice, the following discussion is directed primarily to the parent who is single as the result of divorce.

The Effects of Divorce on Your Children

To understand better the impact of divorce on children, examine some of their feelings. The extent of these feelings will vary depending upon the age of the child, the state of the home before the divorce, and how the divorce was handled by the parents.

Insecurity

The family structure was set up by God so that the child could feel secure in having his needs met appropriately and consistently. Children feel secure in a familiar structure, even though that structure may be a bit shaky. Following a divorce, that structure is removed, and the present and future security of a child is threatened. He or she experiences feelings of uncertainty and loneliness. Young children tend to worry, "Now that Dad has gone, will Mother go, too?" Because the custodial parent, usually the mother, is undergoing a post-divorce adjustment, the capacity to parent is diminished. Most children have so many needs that one parent alone has a difficult time meeting those needs. All these elements work together to intensify the child's insecurity.

Depression

The child of divorce becomes depressed mainly because he feels a sense of loss and a sense of uncertainty about his future care, but the many changes following a divorce also affect him. These may include the loss of a parent's presence in the home, a move to another home or town, the loss of friends, a lessening in financial status, and the stigma of "Mom and Dad are divorced." Although the stigma of divorce is no longer as socially upsetting as it once was, most children perceive that living in a divorced home is not the accepted norm.

Depression manifests itself in different forms according to a child's age and personality. There may be overt signs of depression such as withdrawal, sadness, and multiple psychosomatic complaints (headaches, tummy aches, tiredness). A child may compensate for his depression with "acting-up" behaviors—becoming the class clown, getting into trouble, forming sexual alliances. Some children remain silently depressed and say nothing about the whole situation.

Anger

Children of divorce usually live in a household (or two households) in which anger and resentment persist for several years. A home in which anger predominates diminishes the parent's capacity to be an effective parent and also has a negative effect on a child's developing personality. An angry home will often produce an angry child, and an angry child usually becomes an unhappy and depressed child.

Weakened Self-Esteem

Insecurity, depression, and anger all have a weakening effect on a child's self-esteem. A child with a poor self-esteem is less able to bounce back from the effects of divorce. All of these have a cumulative effect on the child who has no support resources to handle it.

Role Model Loss

Children accustomed to the traditional mother-infant, husband-wife models must adjust to new parental figures. Because both the custodial parent and the absentee parent are now pursuing (either by choice or by necessity) careers outside the home and are coming to terms with their own post-divorce adjustments, the child's expectations of what the traditional mother and father are like are shattered. Not only are his models gone at home, but an older child often gets conflicting messages from his parents. This is particularly true of the absentee parent who may pursue an unchristian lifestyle, which confuses the child who has been taught traditional Christian values. A confused child is susceptible to renouncing the Christian values he has been taught and to departing from the way he should go.

Faith Crisis

The effect of divorce on a Christian child may be even more devastating than for a non-Christian child because in the Christian world, divorce may be considered more a failure than it is in the non-Christian world. The Christian child may therefore become more embarrassed about the divorce. He may turn more closely to his faith or withdraw entirely and pursue an alternative lifestyle. (See the section on the role of the church in divorce for further discussion of the effect of divorce on a Christian child.)

Are boys and girls affected differently by divorce? Although they vary widely in determining how divorce affects either sex, some studies suggest that boys are generally more affected than girls. The reason for this is probably that society encourages boys to suppress their feelings. Boys are discouraged from crying and expressing their sorrows and may choose to vent their stored-up anger in other ways. Girls are more likely to talk freely about what they feel.

Male and female children of divorce differ in their sexual identity problems. Male children of divorce have a higher incidence of homosexuality. Female children of divorce have more sexual problems. Girls often form inappropriate sexual alliances and also marry at a young age to father figures. These sexual identity problems usually result from a loss of appropriate role models.

What happens to children of divorce as they grow older? One cannot generalize or predict accurately the effects of adverse circumstances on a child. In general, however, children of divorce suffer in all areas of life. They have lower academic achievements, more trouble with the law, lower self-esteem, and more problems with sexual identity than children of intact families. But God made children to be resilient, and some children have an immense capacity to bounce back from this family crisis and compensate by actually becoming high achievers. These are tough children. It is interesting that some of the most influential people in the world have come from broken homes.

Effects at Various Stages

1. *Feelings in the preschool child (three to five years).* Preschool children do not usually verbalize their feelings, but they show their resentment by regressive behaviors reflecting insecurity and a sense of loss: thumb-sucking, bed-wetting, whining, temper tantrums, aggressive behaviors, and sleep problems (caused by a fear of awakening and seeing Mommy—or Daddy—gone too). Because of the fear of losing his other parent, the preschool child may cling to his father or mother, crave attention, and not let him or her out of his sight. The young child may also blame himself for the divorce and feel, "I was bad." After the loss of one parent it is common for the preschool child to want to sleep with the custodial parent. This need should be respected during the post-divorce adjustment period.

2. *Feelings of the school-age child (five to ten years).* Children at this age are more likely to verbalize their

feelings and bombard their parents with questions: Why did you divorce? When is Daddy (Mommy) coming back? Children do not accept the finality of divorce, and they fantasize about various ways of reuniting the family. Depression and sadness are part of the grieving process as they come to terms with their loss. The older child usually tries to figure out a reason for the divorce, who the bad guy is, and what is going to happen to him now, especially if there are many changes in lifestyle following the divorce. The child at this age may become angry at one parent or the other. The older child often becomes more sensitive to the loneliness of the custodial parent and may assume the role of friend and companion to the parent. These are healthy roles as long as the compassionate child is allowed to ventilate his feelings while attempting to comfort the grieving parent. Psychosomatic complaints (headaches, stomachaches, fatigue, vague aches and pains) are common during this age and are either attention-getting complaints or real pains related to the body's reaction to the combined stresses. Anticipate a few visits to your child's doctor during the first year following a divorce.

3. *Feelings of the adolescent.* Adolescents are confused. The Christian values they have been taught and the role models they have respected are now weakened. The adolescent may become judgmental about who is at fault and begin to see his parents as individual persons, not as a couple. For this reason, adolescents are very perceptive about how each parent adjusts after the divorce and what lifestyles they choose to pursue. They become particularly judgmental about dating and sexual activities of the parents; therefore, both the mother and the father should exercise some discretion about sexual pursuits. Do not expect your adolescent to warm up immediately to your dates. Because adolescents themselves are going through identity crises, they are particularly vulnerable to the effects of divorce. Adolescents do not usually view divorce as improving the family situation unless there has been excessive physical violence during the marriage.

Whereas the young child is old enough to know what is going on but not old enough to have enough compensatory skills, the adolescent has more support resources to help him cope. Teenage girls may form premature sexual alliances shortly after the divorce because of a need for emotional support and sexual identity. Yes, the adolescent girl is susceptible to pregnancy shortly following the divorce of her parents. Adolescents experience a loyalty dilemma over which parent to support. The way in which this dilemma develops depends upon how each parent reinforces the problem or discourages the adolescent from choosing sides.

Divorce is tough on children of all ages. I do not think it is any tougher at one age than at another; it is simply tough in different ways because children's needs vary at different ages. As the Lord "hates divorce" (Mal. 2:16), so do children of all ages hate divorce.

Common Problems for the Custodial Parent

If the custodial parent is the mother, she may face the conflict between the continuing role of mother and the additional role of worker outside the home. After a divorce it is common for children to increase their demands on the mother's energy and time, and these increased demands come at a time when the mother is also trying to redirect her own life. Most often the mother pursues a career outside the home, for financial reasons and for a psychological boost to her already weakened self-esteem.

Some mothers feel that even though they are not forced to work for financial reasons, it is necessary to pursue some career outside the home for fulfillment as a person. This decision should be made with much prayer and counsel. A custodial mother who is continually unhappy and unfulfilled as a person will not be an effective single parent. Although her primary role will still be that of a mother, it is important for her to do what she has to do for her own individual fulfillment.

My heart goes out to those mothers who are suddenly faced with the dual role of primary breadwinner and loving mother. It is tough to leave one's child in the care of another person, work all day to earn a living for the family, return home from the exhausting world of work, and have energy left over for complete organization of the household. I sincerely believe that God gives a special strength to single mothers who are required to do more than their share.

Discipline

Following a divorce, household routines often become disorganized and discipline relaxed. This is unfortunate because the post-divorce adjustment period is a time when organization and consistent discipline are most needed. This is also a dilemma because the custodial parent may be using so much energy for his or her own adjustment that little is left over for discipline of the child. The following suggestions may help you cope with this dilemma.

As soon as possible after the divorce (or even before), call a family council with your children to give than a clear understanding of the future organization of your home. Even though the home has been severely changed, you are still a family and family life must go on. Older children will have to accept some increased responsibilities. This is a nonnegotiable fact of single-parent family life. The assignment of specific tasks can be negotiated at the family council. Make a list of the new responsibilities to be shared, and let each child have some choice in his or her contribution to the family. Most single parents find it necessary to run a tight ship. Try to achieve some balance between the increased responsibilities that are put upon your children and the emotional support you give them. Too many increased responsibilities too soon may make the already angry child further rebel and resent the divorce. If you increase both your expectations of your child and your show of love for him or her, you child is likely to respect the recent changes in discipline. To avoid the usual confusion of a tight ship at home and a loose ship at Daddy's (or Mother's) house, try to arrive at an agreed-upon level of discipline that will be maintained consistently at each home.

Conflicting Models

A common problem in divorced homes is that children may see alternative lifestyles in their parents' houses. A typical after-divorce scenario is that one parent adopts a free-living lifestyle that he or she demonstrates in front of the child. The child understandably becomes confused. The values he learned from his custodial parent do not match those of the missing parent.

What does a mother do when a child comes to her and asks, "Mommy, is it right for Daddy to be living with another woman?" Mommy is caught in another dilemma. God expects the mother to encourage the child to continue to love his father, yet what the father is doing is clearly wrong. In this case I believe that the mother is obligated to give her child an honest answer: "No, what your father is doing is wrong." When explaining this kind of conflict to your child, try to separate the act from the person: "What Daddy is doing is wrong, but Daddy is not a bad person. You still should love him and pray for him every day that he will again walk with God and do what is right." Taking this approach fulfills your obligation as the spiritual leader of your home and yet, at the same time, encourages your child to love his father.

This problem of conflicting models is intensified further if the child spends prolonged periods of time with one parent, such as during the summer. If this is the case, the custodial parent should spend a great deal of time preparing the child to cope with the alternative lifestyle. If this situation is true for you, intensify your efforts to model Christian values in your own home. Also equip your child with the armor of God. Tell her you will be praying for her each day, and advise her to pray and read Scriptures daily. It would be wise to pick out certain passages of Scripture to serve as a source of strength and direction when she is exposed to alternative values in the house of your ex. (The term *ex* seems cold and final, but really says it all in conveying the anger and resignation that divorced parents often feel.) Encourage your child to call you whenever she feels her faith weakening or is having difficulty accepting these alternative values. Teach your child to go into her father's house not in judgment but in love and strength and prayer.

Helping Children Cope

Once the decision to divorce is final, the way parents handle the divorce is of primary importance. Parents should do all they can to ease the pain for their children.

Tell Them What Is Happening

Parents, do not underestimate your children's ability to understand. Even toddlers have a feeling of not-rightness when one parent is missing. Tell your children a few weeks before the separation occurs, which allows time for questions and feeling to come out during the remaining time the family is intact. Both parents can continue to support the children's adjustment and anxieties. Be specific. Tell your children the reason for the divorce in language and detail appropriate to their age and level of understanding. (Details of marital infidelity serve no useful purpose and should be withheld from them, however.)

It is important for children to feel reassured that they are not the cause of the divorce, that they are still loved, and that they still will have a Mommy and a Daddy, although Daddy (Mommy) will not be living with them. At this point, your children, egocentric as they are, probably will be more concerned about what will happen to them than what will happen to you.

The custodial parent needs to define what changes will occur within the household: Mother will get a job. You will not live in the same house. Children need to be reassured that family life will go on, that family life has not been completely destroyed, only severely changed and adjusted.

It is important for the noncustodial parent to

define what his or her continued role will be in the children's care. This is probably one of the most confusing feelings for children, who at the time are really not sure how much of their parents they will be losing. This is also a dilemma for parents since early in the divorcing period they may not have answered this question in their own minds. Be as specific as possible with your children. Tell them where you are going. If possible, take them to your new home. Leave a phone number and convey one big message: "I am still your dad (mom), and I am easily accessible to you" (if, indeed, you will be so accessible).

After telling your children about the impending divorce, don't be too quick to judge the true meaning of the impact of this crisis on them by their initial reactions. Initially your children may be noncommunicative as they work out their ambivalent feelings concerning this devastating news.

Visiting Rights

During a divorce, parents often are preoccupied with their own "rights." Remember, a child has rights too—a right to two parents. The term *visiting rights* is a superficial term since it implies more fun and entertainment than a relationship. The term *parenting rights* is more realistic and implies more of a commitment to a relationship. Tell your child how often you plan to visit. The younger the child, the more frequent your visits should be. Ideally, visiting a young child should be like his feeding schedule—small, frequent visits on a demand basis. The absentee parent should realize that scheduled parenting is an unrealistic way of life for both you and your child. Weekend parents often schedule lots of fun things, corrective discipline is often lax, and the relationship is that of a "Disneyland parent." This kind of parent-child relationship is not a balanced diet for the growing child. Focus more on giving of yourself than on things; focus more on loving your child than entertaining him or her.

Scheduled parenting is particularly unrealistic for the older child who may have planned his own activities with his own peer group during the weekend you have planned; thus, he will regard your visiting rights as infringing upon his own rights to social development. For the older child, a more flexible, spontaneous, and unscheduled time with the absentee parent respects his busy life, and he should be consulted in working out a visiting arrangement. For example, the father may call up and say, "I would like to be with you tomorrow. What would you like to do?" These visiting dilemmas are not all negative. Parent-child communication may actually improve following a divorce because this may be the first time the child has the parent's undivided attention. Although the concept of quality time is also an artificial relationship, it is really the best the absentee parent can do.

To minimize confusion between the fun-and-games lifestyle with the absentee parent and the more realistic lifestyle in the home of the custodial parent, it would be wise for the absentee parent to point out this artificial relationship to the child by saying, "Johnny, I hope you realize how much I love you and want to spend this fun time with you on weekends. Because I do not have as much time with you as your mother does, we will be doing lots of fun things while we are together. But because I love you, I feel you should understand that life is just not like that all the time. When you are at home with your mother, I expect you to obey and help your mother with the household chores, to complete your homework and do well in school. You know, Johnny, I hope you realize that it is much easier for me than it is for your mother. I can do all my social activities and get my work done during the week so that on the weekend I have time to spend with you. Your mother doesn't have it that easy. She works during the day and is tired at night and may often need the weekends to catch up on some activities that she needs for herself. I want you to realize, son, that if you were living with me and visiting your mother, I would expect the same things from you as what your mother expects at home." You are conveying to your child a more realistic situation.

Make Few Changes

The concept of multiple losses is one of the most difficult problems to cope with. The child has already lost perhaps the most important relationship in his life—a two-parent home. If at all possible, try to keep your child in the same house, the same school, and the same church so that he is not forced to make too many changes too soon. If changes are necessary, try to ease into them gradually; allow the child to adapt to one new relationship at a time.

Protect Your Child

Do not let your child be caught up in the crossfire of hostility between two angry divorcing parents. Do not use your child as a spy or as a carrier of messages. Above all, do not make derogatory remarks about your ex to your child. This only further confuses the child who is trying to sort out his own ambivalent feelings. Consider that the stress of divorce on a child is second only to that following the death of a parent. A confused child is less able to cope with this stress.

Be vigilant for signs that your child is not coping with the divorce, such as depression, acting-up behavior, prolonged anger, the "quiet child" not bothered by anything, poor school performance, fear of forming close friendships, inappropriate sexual alliances, and gradually diminishing self-esteem.

Persons of Significance

Because the child has lost the important model of the intact two-parent home, it is important to help her compensate by surrounding her with other models. These persons of significance could include a pastor, a teacher, a coach, a scout leader—anyone who models for your child the Christian person you want her to be. In a single-parent family, the parent must choose the persons of significance very wisely because the child needs extra help to understand what values are important and which standards should be followed.

Role of the Church

Divorce may be particularly devastating to a Christian couple because they not only have failed a social relationship but they may feel they also have failed a Christian relationship. Divorce is also particularly devastating for the Christian child, since all the ideals he has been taught about the indissolubility of the Christian marriage have been shattered in his own home. For these reasons Christian parents and children may need more support than non-Christians. Unfortunately, this support is not as great as it should be within the Christian community, especially toward divorced parents.

Christians often support the parent who is single because of the death of a spouse, but they may reject a parent who is single because of divorce.

It is also true that a divorced parent does not often seek the fellowship and support within his or her own church because of this feeling of being a failure within the system. A widow or widower has the same practical need but does not feel blamed for being single. A parent single by death may not "feel single"; a parent single by divorce may. Divorced women may have difficulty returning to a state of their own identities, and they may be prone to feelings of loneliness. In some cases parents and children of divorce need more ministering than widows and orphans.

The Bible contains clear instructions that churches and Christian homes should act as extended families to the single parent and the children of single-parent households: "He administers justice for the fatherless and the widow, . . . giving him food and clothing" (Deut. 10:18); "Bring out the tithe of your produce of that year. . . . and the fatherless and the widow who are within your gates, may come and eat and be satisfied" (Deut. 14:28–29); "The LORD watches over . . . and relieves the fatherless and widow" (Ps. 146:9); and "Pure and undefiled religion before God and the Father is this: to visit orphans and widows in their trouble" (James 1:27).

It is extremely important that divorced parents feel their church family has not failed them. The church can help the child of divorce compensate for his loss by taking an active part in his spiritual training. How a child handles a loss or a handicap depends on his degree of compensation. The church family can bring a child closer to God and surround him with Christian models and persons of significance who give the child the message: "We care, and we will not fail you."

Churches often have singles-only Sunday school classes. A word of caution: don't be too quick to suggest to the divorced or widowed parent, "You may want to join the singles class." That parent may not be ready to feel single and may not wish to be ostracized from the fellowship of his or her couples' class and the friends made previously as part of a couple. He or she likes to feel welcomed into couples' activities because of his or her individuality.

The church family also can assist the custodial parent and the children in their grieving process primarily by helping them toward forgiving the absentee parent. Prolonged and stored-up anger is probably one of the greatest obstacles to the post-divorce adjustment. The sooner the custodial parent overcomes this anger and truly says, "I forgive," the sooner he can pull the remaining household together and get on with family life. The most important determinant of how children adjust to divorce is how soon the custodial parent gets both his spiritual house and his earthly house in order.

A message from the church family to parents and children of divorce should be, "We care; we love you as persons, whether single or married; we realize that caring for children takes more than one parent; and we will help you in the material and spiritual care and feeding of both yourself and your children."

I have not been exhaustive of the many challenges that face parents today, but my prayer is that you know *The Sears Parenting Library* is your ally—you are not alone. You have the support of Christian organizations and Christian parents who share your commitment to building a home for God. Above all, you have the promises of Scripture and the continual guidance of our heavenly Father.

As you continue to parent your child and train him in the way he or she should go, remember that your reward will be great, both in this life and in the life to come. I am excited for you; I know that soon you will know your child, will help him or her feel right, and will lead him or her to Christ.

Bibliography

The following books and reference sources are arranged according to their major subjects, although many of them cover a wide range of topics on parenting. Please bear in mind that when recommending a book, *I am not necessarily endorsing every statement made in it.* I have chosen to recommend those books that, in my opinion, contain important messages that will contribute to your growth as Christian parents. Not all of the books on the following list are specifically Christian, but they are not non-Christian either. I have also chosen those books most in accordance with the philosophy of attachment and feeling right that I have continually advocated in this book.

Abortion

Schaeffer, Francis A. and C. Everett Koop. *Whatever Happened to the Human Race?* Westchester, IL: Crossway, 1983.

> Written by the late renowned Christian philosopher and the former surgeon general of the United States, this book is a real must for understanding the issues surrounding abortion, and it exposes the rapid but subtle loss of human rights.

Swindoll, Charles. *Sanctity of Life: The Inescapable Issue.* Dallas, TX: Word, 1990.

> Besides the sanctity of life, Swindoll examines abortion after the fact and makes a plea for morality and the resolve to be strong.

Wilke, Dr. J. C. and Mrs. *Abortion: Questions and Answers*. Cincinnati, OH: Hayes Publishing, 1989.

> If you could choose only one book this should be it: a reference manual with questions and answers on all the aspects of abortion.

Breastfeeding

Breastfeeding Organizations. La Leche League International, Inc., 1-800-LA LECHE, P.O. Box 4079, Schaumberg, IL 60168.

> This organization not only teaches better mothering through breastfeeding but teaches better mothering in all aspects of parenting and child care. There is a local La Leche League in every major city in the United States and throughout the world. Write for a free catalog of their breastfeeding publications, which contains nearly one hundred books and booklets on all aspects of parenting.

Breastfeeding Your Baby: A Mother's Guide.

> A one-hour video produced by Medela, Inc., (the breast pump company) in cooperation with La Leche League. William Sears, M.D., Jay Gordon, M.D., celebrities, and breastfeeding experts instruct and encourage; families speak on breastfeeding's benefits. Available through La Leche League.

Bumgarner, Norma Jane. *Mothering Your Nursing Toddler*. Schaumberg, IL: La Leche League International, Inc., 1982.

> Not only does this book extol the virtues of nursing the toddler and not weaning the child before his time, it is a beautiful account of attachment mothering.

Kippley, Sheila. *Breastfeeding and Natural Child Spacing*. The Couple to Couple League International, Inc., P.O. Box 111184, Cincinnati, OH 45211.

> This book discusses the concept of natural mothering and how it can postpone the return of fertility.

Torgus, Judy, ed. *The Womanly Art of Breastfeeding*. Schaumberg, IL: La Leche League International, Inc., 1987.
   The authority for the breastfeeding mother, this book not only deals with the joys and problems of breastfeeding but also affirms the profession of attachment mothering.

Childbirth

Brewer, Gail Sforza and Tom Brewer, M.D. *What Every Pregnant Woman Should Know: The Truth About Diet and Drugs in Pregnancy*. New York: Viking-Penguin, 1985.
   The importance of good nutrition in pregnancy. Relationship of toxemia and diet in pregnancy.

Dick-Read, Grantly. *Childbirth Without Fear*. (5th ed.) Edited by Helen Wessel. New York: Harper and Row, 1984.
   This is a classic book on natural childbirth that demonstrates how laboring women can overcome the fear-tension-pain cycle.

Evans, Debra. *The Complete Book on Childbirth*. Wheaton, IL: Tyndale House, 1986.
   This book is valuable for the original and beautifully expressed concepts on marriage and birth. Her information on breastfeeding is insufficient and I do not completely agree with her attitudes toward pain and childbirth. Readers will want to balance this book with others on Christian childbirth and breastfeeding.

Korte, Diana and Roberta Scaer. *A Good Birth, A Safe Birth*. New York: Bantam, 1990.
   This basic guide to childbirth options helps expectant parents negotiate to get the kind of birth experience they want. Also provides insight into recent trends in childbirth.

MacNutt, Francis and Judith. *Praying for Your Unborn Child: How Parents' Prayers Can Make a Difference in the*

Health and Happiness of Their Children. New York: Doubleday, 1989.

A beautiful and insightful guide to praying for your baby during each stage of pregnancy, from conception to delivery. The authors show how parents who surround their unborn infant with love, prayer, and serenity will profoundly affect their child's personality and well-being.

McCutcheon-Rosegg, Susan and Peter Rosegg. *Natural Childbirth the Bradley Way.* New York: E. P. Dutton-Penguin, 1984.

An updated guide to pregnancy and childbirth. Step-by-step preparations are provided for the couple looking for a totally natural, drug-free birth.

Nilsson, Lennart. *A Child Is Born.* (Rev. ed.) New York: Delacourt, 1990. Also published by Life Education, reprint no. 27. Canaan, NH: Media International.

A series of unprecedented photographs of the development of the embryo, from conception to birth, the book will help you realize the true miracle of fetal development and how a Supreme Architect is certainly in charge of this development.

Noble, Elizabeth. *Having Twins: A Parent's Guide to Pregnancy, Birth and Early Childhood.* Boston, MA: Houghton-Mifflin, 1991.

A veteran childbirth expert tells how to carry healthy babies to term.

Odent, Michael, M.D. *Birth Reborn.* New York: Random House, 1984.

A beautifully illustrated description of birth at Pithiviers in France, using explicit photography to help demonstrate how birth is best achieved in the modified (standing) squat position and also with the aid of tubs. The description of how birth can be a normal, safe, and confident part of life encourages couples in planning the birth they want.

Sears, William M. and Linda H. Holt. *The Pregnancy Book: A Month-by-Month Guide*. New York: Little Brown Co., 1997.

Wessel, Helen. *Natural Childbirth and the Christian Family*. Bookmates International, Inc., Apple Tree Family Ministries, P.O. Box 2083, Artesia, CA 90702–2083, 562-925-0149.
> A must for all parents who are taking prepared-childbirth classes. Mrs. Wessel, a mother of six, adds a Christian perspective to the childbirth-without-fear techniques described by Dr. Grantly Dick-Read.

_____. *Under the Apple Tree*. Fresno, CA: Bookmates International, Inc., 1982. (See above for address to write for booklet.)
> An absolute must for Christian parents-to-be. Mrs. Wessel discusses the scriptural basis of marriage, birthing, and early parenting practices; it should be read and studied by husband and wife together.

Discipline

Craig, Sydney. *Raising Your Child Not by Force but by Love*. Philadelphia, PA: The Westminster Press, 1973.
> This book, written from a Christian perspective, helps parents gain an understanding of discipline as a *positive* concept. It has great insight into the feelings of children and the effect of our discipline (good and bad) on their feelings. It also gives insight into why we get angry with our children and alternative ways of expressing and managing anger.

Crary, Elizabeth. *Without Spanking or Spoiling*. Seattle, WA: Parenting Press, 1979.
> Alternatives for parents to recognize and attain their personal goals in childrearing.

_____. *Kids Can Cooperate: A Practical Guide to Teaching Problem Solving*. Seattle, WA: Parenting Press, 1984.
> Teaches children skills to solve conflicts themselves.

_____. *Pick Up Your Socks . . . And Other Skills Growing Children Need*. Seattle, WA: Parenting Press, 1990.
Teaches children responsibility skills.

Faber, Adele and Elaine Mazlish. *Siblings Without Rivalry*. New York: Avon, 1987.
Help your children live together so you can live too.

_____. *How to Talk So Kids Will Listen and Listen So Kids Will Talk*. New York: Avon, 1982.
Communication skills for parents: how to listen and deal with feelings; alternatives to nagging and punishment.

Fennema, Jack. *Nurturing Children in the Lord*. Phillipsburg, NJ: Presbyterian and Reformed Publishing, 1977.
A study guide on developing a biblical approach to discipline, this is an excellent book for Christian parents who wish to base their discipline on scriptural principles.

Kesler, Jay. *Too Big to Spank*. Ventura, CA: Regal, 1978.
This is a practical guide for parents to help them discipline and build self-esteem in their teenager.

Leman, Kevin. *Making Children Mind Without Losing Yours*. Old Tappan, NJ: Revell, 1984.
Should have been titled *Helping Children Mind* by Dr. Leman's own admission. A practical, commonsense approach to discipline based on action (but rarely spanking), not words. Called Reality Discipline, it teaches children to be accountable for their actions. Only one area of concern: Dr. Leman advises parents to leave their young babies at home so they can get out now and then. I encourage couples to get out together and take baby too.

Narramore, S. Bruce. *Help! I'm a Parent*. Grand Rapids, MI: Zondervan, 1972.

This book applies both psychological and biblical principles in arriving at a systematic approach to discipline.

Sears, William M. and Martha Sears. *The Discipline Book: Everything You Need to Know to Have a Better Behaved Child*. New York: Little Brown Co., 1995.

Stewart, Blaize Clement. *The Loving Parent: A Guide to Growing Up Before Your Children Do*. San Luis Obispo, CA: Impact, 1988.
A secular book dealing sensitively with issues such as obedience, lying, stealing, cheating, anger, and sexuality.

Divorce

Hart, Archibald D. *Children and Divorce—What to Expect, How to Help*. Waco, TX: Word, 1982.
Written by a Christian psychologist, this realistic and helpful guidebook helps divorcing parents understand their children's feelings and help them cope.

Smith, Virginia Watts. *The Single Parent*. Old Tappan, NJ: Revell, 1979.
This very sensitive Christian guide to the plight of the single parent offers sympathetic understanding and practical advice on the dilemma of achieving personal fulfillment and rearing a child for Christ.

Education

Elkind, David. *The Hurried Child, Growing Up Too Fast, Too Soon*. Reading, MA: Addison-Wesley, 1989.
Offers insight and advice on the burden of stress on modern children who are "forced to bloom."

Harris, Gregg. *The Christian Home School*. Brentwood, TN: Wolgemuth & Hyatt, 1987.
A good starter book for families considering home school.

Macauley, Susan Schaeffer. *For the Children's Sake: Foundations of Education for Home and School.* Westchester, IL: Crossway, 1987.

The daughter of the late Christian philosopher Francis A. Schaeffer, who grew up in Switzerland and L'Abri Fellowship, writes about the wonderful, life-enriching, joyous experience education can be for your child, in your home and in school.

Montessori, Maria. *The Discovery of the Child.* New York: Ballantine, 1967.

A good explanation of the Montessori philosophy of education, this book defines the needs and offers practical education suggestions for the various sensitive periods of the child.

Moore, Raymond S. and Dorothy N. *Home Grown Kids.* Waco, TX: Word, 1981.

A practical handbook for teaching your children at home, this book calls attention to the fact that education is still the prime responsibility of the parent. The educational suggestions are provocative and well worth considering; however, I do not agree with some of the authors' suggestions on early child care, especially much of their nutritional advice.

Sears, William M. and L. Thompson. *The A.D.D. Book: Attention Deficit Disorder.* New York: Little Brown Co., 1998.

Uphoff, James K., June E. Gilmore, and Rosemarie Huber. *Summer Children—Ready or Not for School.* J & J Publishing Co., P.O. Box 8549, Middletown, OH 45042.

Marriage

Crabb, Lawrence Jr. *How to Become One with Your Mate.* Grand Rapids, MI: Zondervan, 1982.

This is a small, very readable excerpt from *The Marriage Builder,* by Lawrence Crabb, on oneness of body and spirit in the marriage relationship. Looking to

Christ to fulfill our needs enables us to minister to our mates.

Harley, Willard. *His Needs, Her Needs: Building an Affair-Proof Marriage*. Old Tappan, NJ: Revell, 1986.
Identifies the ten most important marital needs of husbands and wives and teaches how those needs can be fulfilled.

Wheat, Ed, M.D. and Gloria Okes Perkins. *Love Life for Every Married Couple*. Grand Rapids, MI: Zondervan, 1980.
How to fall in love, stay in love, rekindle your love.

Media

Farah, Joseph (editor). *Between the Lines*. 325 Pennsylvania Ave., SE, Washington, DC 20003.
A biweekly newsletter covering the politics and morality of the news media and entertainment industry.

Lappe, Francis Moore. *What to Do After You Turn Off the TV*. New York: Ballantine, 1985.

For other information concerning media write:

Christian Leaders for Responsible Television
c/o American Family Association
P.O. Box 2440
Tupelo, MS 38803

Mother-Infant Attachment

Fraiberg, Selma. "Every Child's Birthright." In *Selected Writings of Selma Fraiberg*. Louis Fraiberg, editor. Columbus, OH: Ohio State University Press, 1987.

Kaplan, Louise. *Oneness and Separateness: From Infant to Individual*. New York: Simon and Schuster, 1978.
A beautiful discussion of the inner workings of the child as he goes from oneness to separateness. Dr. Kaplan explores some of the theory of the benefits of mother-infant attachment and the consequences of premature detachment.

Klaus and Kennell. *Parent-Infant Bonding*. Saint Louis, MO: C. V. Mosby, 1982.

This book discusses results of studies that suggest the positive benefits of mother and baby remaining in close contact with each other immediately after birth.

McClure, Vimala Schneider. *Infant Massage*. New York: Bantam, 1989.

Teaches parents to discover the joys and benefits of massage for their babies and for themselves. Photographs illustrate each step of the process. Massage promotes bonding, reduces tension and fussing, and aids in physical development. I highly recommend this book.

Montagu, Ashley. *Touching: The Human Significance of the Skin*. New York: Harper and Row, 1986.

The classical treatise on the importance of the skin as the largest organ of human sensation. Dr. Montagu discusses at length the psychological benefits of skin-to-skin contact.

Natural Family Planning

Kass-Annese, Barbara, R.N., N.P., and Hal Danzer, M.D. *The Fertility Awareness Workbook*. New York: Putnam, 1981.

A concise, how-to book on natural family planning. Good illustrations and diagrams.

Kippley, Sheila. *Breastfeeding and Natural Child Spacing*. Cincinnati, OH: The Couple to Couple League International, Inc., 1989.

This book discusses the concept of natural mothering and how it can postpone the return of fertility.

Kippley, John and Sheila. *The Art of Natural Family Planning*. Cincinnati, OH: The Couple to Couple League International, Inc., 1989.

To be used either on your own or as part of an instructional program, the book teaches the symptothermal method of fertility control. Part One explains the "why" of NFP; Part Two the "how to." My favorite chapter is entitled "Marriage Building with NFP."

New Age

Kjos, Barit. *Your Child and the New Age.* Wheaton, IL: Victor, 1990.

A solid explanation of various aspects of the New Age influence in schools and media, with practical suggestions on what parents can do. Issues such as counterfeit spirituality, values clarification, New Age globalism in schools, mind manipulation, distortion of imagination, pagan sentiments in toys, TV, movies, reading material, and music.

Michaelsen, Johanna. *Like Lambs to the Slaughter: Your Child and the Occult.* Eugene, OR: Harvest House, 1989.

Information parents need to have to help their children survive or avoid the subtle and not-so-subtle New Age influences in the world today.

Parenting and Child Care

Cahill, Mary Ann. *The Heart Has Its Own Reasons.* New York: New American Library, 1985.

This book encourages mothers to stay home with their children and gives practical and timely suggestions on how that can be managed financially.

Campbell, D. Ross. *How to Really Love Your Child.* Wheaton, IL: Victor, 1978.

This book, written by a Christian psychiatrist, discusses the importance of touching, eye-to-eye contact, and focused attention. It offers practical tips on how to convey your love to your child.

_____. *How to Really Love Your Teenager.* Wheaton, IL: Victor, 1981.

Encouraging guidance for parents struggling to understand and express love to their teens. Picks up where *How to Really Love Your Child* leaves off.

Crook, William G. and Laura J. Stevens. *Solving the Puzzle of Your Hard to Raise Child.* New York: Random House, 1987.
Parents of high-need children need the information in this book concerning the effect on behavior of improper or inadequate nutrition. Tells how to improve the child's diet and, therefore, his behavior.

Dobson, James. *Hide or Seek.* Tappan, NJ: Revell, 1979.
In my opinion this is the best of Dr. Dobson's many books. It deals with the extremely important issue of how to build self-esteem in your child.

_____. *Preparing for Adolescence.* New York: Bantam, 1980.
An excellent text for parent and preteen to share, with an accompanying study guide for your child. I've used it as each of our first four approached their teen years.

Noble, Elizabeth. *Having Twins: A Parent's Guide to Pregnancy, Birth, and Early Childhood.* Boston, MA: Houghton-Mifflin, 1991.
A veteran childbirth expert tells how to carry healthy babies to term.

Sears, William M. and Martha Sears. *The Baby Book: Everything You Need to Know About Your Baby—From Birth to Age Two.* New York: Little Brown Co., 1993.

_____. *Becoming a Father: How to Nurture and Enjoy Your Family.* Schaumberg, IL: La Leche League International, 1986.

_____. *Growing Together: A Parents' Guide to Baby's First Year.* Schaumberg, IL: La Leche League International, 1987.
This book describes the month-by-month development of babies from birth to one year.

————. *Nighttime Parenting*. Schaumberg, IL: La Leche League International, 1987.
Practical tips for parenting your child to sleep.

————. *Parenting the Fussy Baby and High Need Child*. New York: Little Brown Co., 1996.

————. *SIDS: A Parent's Guide to Understanding and Preventing the Sudden Infant Death Syndrome*. New York: Little Brown Co., 1995.

Sex Education

Andry, Andrew and Stephen Schepp. *How Babies Are Made*. New York: Little-Brown, 1984.
This is the perfect starter book for teaching the reproductive process to your children. Illustrated with paper sculpture, figures are realistic and simple. Begins with plants and animals, and tastefully illustrates humans, for ages 3–10. Ends with the mother breastfeeding her baby.

Kitzinger, Sheila and Lennart Nilsson. *Being Born*. New York: Grosset Dunlap, 1986.
The same magnificent photos of Nilssons's *A Child Is Born* combined with poetic text about conception and birth make this book timeless. Adults as well as children are drawn to it, even though it is written for children.

McDowell, Josh and Dick Day. *Why Wait? What You Need to Know About the Teen Sexuality Crisis*. San Bernardino, CA: Here's Life Publishers, 1987.
A very frank look at the situation challenging teens and the biblical perspective on what God wants for their lives in regard to chastity.

Sexuality

Evans, Debra. *The Mystery of Womanhood*. Westchester, IL: Crossway, 1987.

A biblical perspective on being a woman, finding the inner beauty of femininity, handling stress of daily living, fertility and childbearing, sexuality in a healthy marriage, and living with a cyclical nature.

Penner, Clifford and Joyce. *The Gift of Sex: A Christian Guide to Sexual Fulfillment*. Waco, TX: Word, 1981.
A comprehensive and joyful guide to sex for Christians.

Sleep Problems

Sears, William. *Nighttime Parenting*. Schaumberg, IL: La Leche League International, 1987.
Practical tips for parenting your child to sleep.

Thevenin, Tine. *The Family Bed*. New York: Avery, 1987.
This book brings back an age-old concept in child rearing and advocates children sleeping with their parents or with other siblings as a way to solve bedtime problems, create a closer bond within the family, and give children a greater sense of security.

Your Child's Devotional Life

Blitchington, Evelyn. *The Family Devotions Idea Book*. Minneapolis, MN: Bethany House, 1982.
This book is full of practical ideas on how to conduct meaningful family devotions.

Chapin, Alice. *Building Your Child's Faith*. Nashville, TN: Thomas Nelson, 1990.
Simple, fun ideas for teaching children how to pray, worship, and discover the Bible.

Haystead, Wes. *Teaching Your Child About God*. Ventura, CA: Regal, 1981.
This is an easy-to-read book with practical advice on the spiritual training of the child at various stages.

Index

About the Authors

William Sears, M.D., and his wife, Martha Sears, R.N., have more than two decades of professional pediatric experience. Dr. Sears is clinical assistant professor of pediatrics at the University of Southern California School of Medicine and a practicing pediatrician. Martha Sears is a registered nurse and a certified childbirth educator.

They have cared for more than ten thousand babies, including eight of their own. Dr. Sears has written twelve books on raising children, including five with his wife.

LOOK FOR THESE OTHER BOOKS IN THE SEARS PARENTING LIBRARY

So You're Going To Be A Parent
Practical advice for the soon-to-be mom and dad. Provides information on healthy living during pregnancy, as well as what to expect during and after the delivery.

0-7852-7206-2 • 216 pages • Mass Market Paperback

Now That Baby Is Home
Learn about your baby's emotional and physical needs, while developing a parenting style that works in your family.

0-7852-7207-0 • 276 pages • Mass Market Paperback